Practical Workforce Planning
for
HR Professionals

Brian Allen

Gravitas Publishing
Taupo. New Zealand.

Brian Allen / Gravitas Publishing
gravitas1@vodafone.co.nz

Practical Workforce Planning for HR Professionals. Brian Allen —1st ed.
ISBN 978-1542772952

Contents

5

Preface

"I imagine workforce planning to be rather like a weather forecast. We may not be able to predict exactly how many inches of rain will fall, but we can still make a decision as to whether or not it is a good idea to go for a picnic." Alexandra Chauran.

Jack Welch has famously said *"if the rate of change inside your firm is slower than the rate of change occurring outside your firm, your end is in sight"*. This observation is confirmed by the litany of business disasters due, most obviously, to a failure to adapt and keep moving ahead.

This is all very well, but the ability to change rapidly, to be agile and nimble is mostly directly proportional to the scale of an organization. The elephant is inevitably more ponderous than the flea. We could argue that small businesses do not need to immerse themselves in time-consuming workforce forecasting exercises. They can operate well enough at the edge of chaos. Larger scale businesses, on the other hand, cannot function without some degree of prediction because their ability to compensate for a lack of foresight must be longer term and will require greater resource.

While there are certainly businesses whose core operations shift only slowly, change that impacts on the numbers of staff required, either by way of reductions or increases, is inevitable. It is undoubtedly true that if businesses are to manage risk responsibly they must, to some degree, take on the task of continuously anticipating the scale and nature of change that will impact them and attempt to forecast their optimum workforce quantum and composition. The difficulties involved in such crystal ball gazing are increasingly compounded by the exponentially increasing rate of change and the inability (of most of us) to make sense of the apparent chaos.

The concept of the VUCA world has certainly come of age. First used by the American military in the 1950's to describe the mounting global uncertainties emerging from the onset of the cold war, VUCA is now common parlance among organizational strategists and planners who acknowledge that the world is evermore:

> Volatile – situations are likely to change suddenly, unpredictably and probably for the worse.
>
> Uncertain – nothing can be assumed or taken for granted.
>
> Complex – the range of factors that must be considered may move beyond the organization's ability to process or model rationally.
>
> Ambiguous – most situations now lend themselves to various interpretations.

Contemporary management thinking now tells us that we have to get comfortable with 'living at the edge of chaos', and it is those organizations that learn to exploit this VUCA world that will survive and thrive. The recipe for success now calls for businesses to be 'agile' and 'nimble' and to pursue change more or less for its own sake.

So the question for larger scale enterprises is "how do we achieve a meaningful level of prediction around our workforce needs?" Accepting that prediction and forecasting in a VUCA world can never be an exact science, businesses and their HR departments have a number of options at their disposal. They may adopt one, or perhaps more sensibly, use a combination, depending on their particular context, skills, resources and the richness of available data.

The purpose of this short book is to describe some of the relatively simple, internally designed approaches by which HR departments can achieve a reasonably confident forecast of future workforce needs, and thus go on to plan more strategically to meet business needs. HR professionals are not statisticians. Consequently we cannot expect them to employ the complex algorithmic or stochastic modeling used at government level to predict whole of workforce trends. Furthermore, it is doubtful that those techniques would provide the locally sensitive perspective that individual businesses (or individual workplaces) undoubtedly need.

Consequently, this book focuses on describing practical tools that HR departments can adopt and adapt according to their specific needs and context. These are resources that can easily be developed and used in-house avoiding the need for costly software options that, in practice are unlikely to offer complete solutions.

1

What is Workforce Planning?

As organizations grapple with increasing complexity and uncertainty, they naturally gravitate toward any device that might provide an additional element of clarity. Having a 'plan' brings with it at least a sensation of control, no matter how fleeting. Chief among the uncertainties, we are told, is the emerging crisis of skills shortages in the developed world. The ability to attract the best talent is heralded as the principal differentiator between future success or indeed, of future failure.

Consequently, we should not be surprised that the concept of 'workforce planning' has emerged as a contemporary business imperative, and, it is indeed undergoing a relative renaissance from its 1980's inception as 'manpower planning', undertaken in the old 'personnel departments'. The chief problem for the HR professional is that there appears to be no absolute consensus concerning either the objectives or the methodologies of workforce planning. It is my contention that this is a virtue rather than a vice. One size will not fit all. Nevertheless we will need some kind of standard definition. What does this re-emerging phenomenon entail?

The Chartered Institute of Personnel and Development (CIPD) provides a succinct answer to this question:

Workforce planning is a process to ensure the right number of people, with the right skills are employed in the right place at the right time to deliver an organization's short and long-term objectives. It embraces a diverse and extensive range of activities which will vary between organizations and situations. These activities may include:

- *Succession planning*
- *Flexible working*
- *Labour demand and supply forecasting*
- *Recruitment and retention planning*
- *Skills audit gap analysis*
- *Talent management*
- *Multi-skilling*
- *Job design*
- *Outsourcing*
- *Risk management*
- *Career planning*
- *Scenario planning* (1)

While this somewhat prosaic description provides an insight into related processes and activities, it is, to my mind, fundamentally flawed in as much as it suggests that all these listed activities serve the workforce planning process. We are led to believe that 'talent management' is a sub-set of workforce planning, when, in fact the opposite is true. The right people, with the right skills, in the right place, at the right time, is more accurately a description of talent management, and workforce planning is a functional sub-set of that overarching process.

Figure 1.1 below, illustrates how workforce planning processes 'kick-start' the talent management cycle by identifying the roles that need to be maintained, transitioned or acquired to service the organizational strategic business plan.

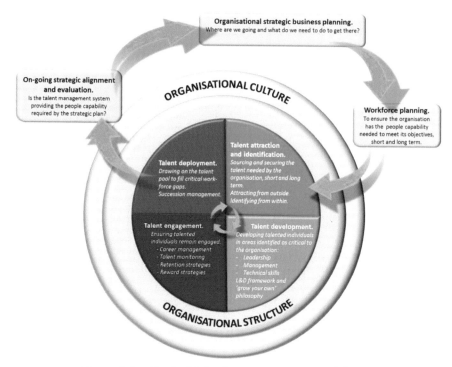

Figure 1.1 – Typical talent management model.

It will be clear from this model that the workforce plan must be a living process, constantly responsive to the organization's strategic planning. The strategic planning cycle must provide clear direction on where the organization is headed, how it intends to get there and who will be needed to ensure it reaches its destination. The reference to 'who' takes us back to the CIPD concept i.e. 'right people, with right skills, at the right time, in the right place'. Consequently, the link between strategic planning and workforce planning is critical. If senior management cannot provide a continually updated view of the quantum and quality of people it will need to move forward (both for business as usual operations and for new initiatives), the ultimate effectiveness of workforce planning will inevitably be diminished. As we move into a potentially prolonged era of skills shortages and workforce depletion through 'boomer' retirement, the need for senior management and HR to be on top of their game increases significantly day by day.

Figure 1.1. positions workforce planning as the 'front end' of the talent management cycle. Until HR has clear direction on the numbers and kinds of people required, the talent attraction and recruitment processes cannot begin. We should not forget, however, that the workforce plan will also address and support other parts of the cycle; especially the effective deployment of existing employees and the succession planning process.

Interrogating the strategic plan.

Clarity of direction is of course the stuff of strategy. HR cannot plan effectively without access to the business strategic plan and, preferably being directly involved in the strategic planning process. A professional HR presence in the senior management team is critical in this respect.

We should not necessarily assume that all organizations will produce strategic plans. Of course they *should* – but in practice many (particularly smaller organizations) will either lack the expertise or regard the process as burdensome bureaucracy, getting in the way of actually doing the job. Strategic planning is the process of engaging with the future and plotting your way to specific destinations. The most successful and long-lasting businesses are constantly gazing into the crystal ball. Those that function only at the tactical level eventually court disaster. As the Chinese general Sun Tzu put it:

> *Strategy without tactics is the slowest route to victory – but tactics without strategy is just the noise before defeat.*

In other words those businesses that become entirely focused on day to day operations, without keeping an eye on the horizon are most likely doomed to failure. Business strategy will focus principally on what needs to be achieved i.e. business goals and objectives. Strategic plans will seldom open up to a level of detail that includes specifying the kinds of people needed to achieve those goals. Indeed, many would say they should not, because that is the stuff of tactical /operational planning. It falls to the HR professionals therefore to draw this information out of senior managers e.g. what kind of people do we need and how many i.e. capability and capacity? It is easy to see that without a properly articulated strategic plan, answering these questions is, at best, no more than educated guesswork.

Mapping and profiling roles.

Once required roles are identified the question arises 'what is the individual in this role actually required to do?' The answer is properly provided through functional analysis. This provides a clear picture of the tasks and activities that the individual will be called upon to perform and, subsequently, of the knowledge, skills and experience that are needed to ensure success in the role.

Role *mapping* is a precise process aimed at a full depth analysis of work that is entirely predictable and linked to fixed routines. Consequently role maps tend to be associated with lower level functions such as production operatives.

Role *profiling* differs significantly in as much as it focuses on roles that are not so predictable and require greater flexibility and adaptability to changing circumstances. Functional description is limited more to higher level descriptions. Greater detail accompanies the description of knowledge, skills experience and attributes. Role profiles are therefore more suited to roles such as managers, engineers, and other professionals. Attempts to be prescriptive in defining these roles usually meet with resistance.

Role maps and role profiles are of obvious significance at the recruiting stage of the talent management cycle. They are also critical to the development of the individual as he or she progresses from role to role. After all, if you do not know, in depth, what the individual is expected to do, you cannot train or develop him to do it.

Aligning behaviours.

Of course functional analysis is not sufficient, on its own, to define the requirements for a given role. *What* somebody does is only part of the equation. We also need to define *how* the individual should go about their tasks and achieving their targets. What is needed is an analysis of the *behaviours* we expect the individual to demonstrate as they fulfill their responsibilities. For example, it is not sufficient simply to set a sales person a year-end target (the *what)* without communicating clear expectations in terms of behavioural standards (the *how*). Without such clear understanding, we should not be entirely surprised if the achievement of sales targets is accompanied by unethical behaviour.

These behavioural requirements are most often embedded in *competency* frameworks. Competencies may be attached to, or form an integral part of both role maps and role profiles. Once again, behavioural competencies will play a highly significant part in recruitment and identifying suitability of 'fit' for specific roles. They can be directly referenced to support the behavioural question components of selection interviewing.

Risk prediction and management via heat mapping.

Businesses globally are facing up to the challenges of skills shortages and the potential loss of institutional knowledge as the baby boomer 'silver tsunami' exits the workforce. The situation is far worse in those industries dependent on high levels of technical knowledge and skill. As long-serving employees leave the organization they will take with them valuable, perhaps even critical intellectual capital. HR must find a way to predict, with reasonable reliability, the exit patterns, peaks and troughs, far enough into the future to be sure of minimizing the significant risk posed by inadequate succession planning.

Key to such risk mitigation is the identification of the 'hot spots' i.e. the roles regarded as being of significant value that are moving toward retirement either through age or for medical reasons. In addition, HR must monitor the bigger picture at whole of workforce level, in order to understand the numbers likely to exit the business year on year and thus identify the chronological hot spots.

'Heat mapping' of this kind is only possible if good historical HR data is available. A good human resources information system (HRIS) should allow the mining of data that can be extrapolated into the future to provide a basis for forecasting.

Prioritization of resources to critical roles.

Even a cursory analysis of organizational performance will reveal that certain roles are more significant for success. For example, a manufacturing business may cite the front line supervisor role as a critical and pivotal function - not only because of the obvious need to manage the 'coal face' efficiently, but also because this role is the principal portal for the transmission of organizational values and cultural norms to the wider workforce.

These critical roles will vary between organizations and quite possibly from time to time within the same entity. What matters is that management must be aware of these criticalities, identify the roles and ensure that every effort is made to ensure succession into them. In essence this is a 3-dimensionalizing of the workforce. In practice these tend to be the more senior roles, largely due to the knowledge and skills locked up in those individuals and the time it takes to bring replacements up to speed. Nevertheless, more junior roles can become critical if, for example, processes change or the 'lemming effect' leads to a wholesale exit of staff from a specific role.

Critical Role Analysis (CRA) must be an ongoing part of the workforce planning process. Organizations need to question their micro-environment continually, looking at each component of their operations and asking "the loss of which individual / role would hurt us the most at the moment?"

Workforce planning – the playing field.

It is useful to think of workforce planning as having 3 continually active 'horizons'. Figure 1.2 below illustrates these. In most organizations strategic planning is the distant 'blue' horizon, at least 2 – 5 years out, but in our VUCA world many businesses will find that kind of projection very difficult. Consequently, strategic plans will need frequent reviews and updates to remain relevant. To work effectively in this rarified atmosphere we need guidance from the organizational strategic plan and from our own environmental scanning. The task, at this level, is primarily to translate strategic intention into people equivalents, both in terms of the numbers, skills and specific competencies needed, and which roles should be prioritized due to their relative criticality for business success.

Closer in to the present, we are working at the tactical level, looking to the 'green' horizon. 1-2 years out we should have firmed up the people needs from blue horizon analysis. The focus in this area is grounded in recruitment tactics, ensuring that we have critical roles covered by adequate succession plans and that those coming through the 'pipeline' have access to appropriate induction and learning.

'Red' horizon workforce planning barely qualifies as a true planning activity. In reality we are talking about reaction to events upsetting the green horizon plan. We can think of this as normal stresses and tensions that occur, day to day, within the workforce dynamic. Consequently, what we see generally is 'firefighting' in the form of rework-ing rosters, short term transfers or secondments between teams etc.

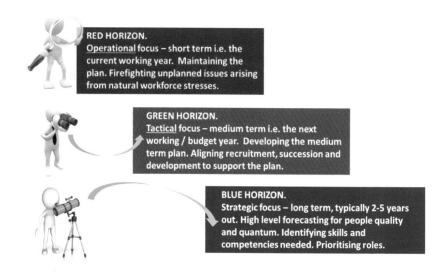

RED HORIZON.
Operational focus – short term i.e. the current working year. Maintaining the plan. Firefighting unplanned issues arising from natural workforce stresses.

GREEN HORIZON.
Tactical focus – medium term i.e. the next working / budget year. Developing the medium term plan. Aligning recruitment, succession and development to support the plan.

BLUE HORIZON.
Strategic focus – long term, typically 2-5 years out. High level forecasting for people quality and quantum. Identifying skills and competencies needed. Prioritising roles.

Figure 1.2 – Workforce planning horizons.

Summary.

Workforce planning is therefore the attempt to ensure that the talent management cycle is aligned appropriately to organizational strategy. It operates at various stages around the cycle and supports numerous HR and management functions through the provision of targeted analysis of workforce continuity or necessary innovation.

As long ago as 2002 *Workforce* magazine highlighted the importance of workforce planning:

Being prepared is better than being surprised. Workforce planning is a sys-tematic, fully integrated organizational process that involves proactively planning ahead to avoid talent surpluses or shortages. It is based on the premise that a company can be staffed more efficiently if it forecasts its talent needs as well as the actual supply of talent that is or will be available.

Business people who just wait and then attempt to react to current events will not thrive for very long. The new standard is to provide managers with warnings and action plans to combat full-blown problems before they become more than a blip on their radar. The HR world is no different. The rate of change in the talent market is dramatic. We now know how important talent is to the success of a business. It's time to make the talent pipeline (a defined recruiting channel where a company can find qualified talent to meet its specific needs) more efficient. It's also time to manage your talent inventory (a company's current employee base) so that there isn't a shortage or a surplus. (2)

So, if it is this important, why, in 2016, in so many organizations, is workforce planning still an afterthought, if it is a thought at all? Despite the now pressing need for fully developed systems many organizations (including their HR departments) continue to procrastinate and offer a litany of reasons for doing so. The usual excuses include:

- *'Not enough time – we are too busy with everything else'.*
- *'Not enough expertise – this stuff is too complicated without using external consultants'.*
- *'This is too far out. We need to focus on year end results. We can't see the immediate gains from this'.*
- *'Not enough data for any analysis to be meaningful'.* Of course this may be a genuine situation.
- *'We've got things under control. We don't need all this statistical stuff – our gut feelings are sufficient'.*
- *'We don't know what level of analysis we should use or which parts of the business need it'.*
- *'Analysis paralysis – we've tried it and we just get bogged down in all the detail. Nothing concrete ever comes of it'.*

The reality here is most likely that so many HR professionals are incorrectly advised that workforce planning is a daunting and time-consuming exercise, the results of which senior management are unlikely to understand anyway. It is my belief that much can be achieved through the use of relatively straightforward tools and techniques that produce results that management can readily comprehend and embrace. In short, it does not need to be 'rocket science'.

We will go on to look at some of these essential workforce planning processes in more depth.

References.

1. CIPD Fact Sheet October 2015. Available at *http://www.cipd.co.uk/hr-resources/factsheets/workforce-planning.aspx*
2. Sullivan D. (2002) *Why you need workforce planning*. Workforce magazine.

2

Forecasting – options available for HR

A global context.

As the 'silver tsnunami' of retiring baby boomers rolls out through the plant gates, they would, all things being equal, naturally be replaced by the succeeding "Gen Xers'. But of course all things are not equal. Generation X, in the developed world, is significantly smaller in numbers than its predecessor. The normal patterns of succession are being seriously disrupted by a simple shortage of bodies. When we add in to that equation the factor of inappropriate or non-existent skills (as described in the ongoing STEM/STEAM debate) (1), a yawning gap begins to appear. In time we anticipate, hopefully, that the chasm will be bridged, in terms of numbers, by the millennials coming through - although in countries with diminishing birth rates such as Japan, this is not likely to happen. In any case, the skills issue remains.

The 2015 Manpower Group *Talent Shortage Survey* (2) highlighted the seriousness of the issues.
- Globally, nearly 40 % of all companies are experiencing real difficulties filling roles.
- The 10 most difficult roles to fill are:
    - Skilled trades workers

- Skilled sales reps
- Engineers
- Technicians
- Heavy goods vehicle drivers
- Managers / Executives
- Accounting / Finance staff
- Office support staff
- IT staff
- Production / machine operators

The principal reasons behind these difficulties are:

- Lack of available applicants / no applicants - 35% of companies
- Lack of technical competencies (hard skills) – 34% of companies
- Lack of appropriate experience – 22% of companies
- Lack of workplace competencies (soft skills) – 17% of companies
- Seeking higher salaries than those offered – 13% of companies.

Despite this increasingly precarious situation many organizations are still doing little or nothing to get to grips with a planned response. As Madeline Laurano, Principal Analyst with Bersin & Associates Research points out *"the majority of workforce planning processes are conducted on an 'as needed' basis. They address the current headcount, but fail to help business leaders plan for the skills and core competencies needed in the future".* (3) Scanning the horizon reveals that those companies that have engaged in workforce planning processes are travelling on a journey through 4 levels of 'maturity' from simple headcount replacement to a sophisticated blend of alignment with business strategy, internal skills development planning, strategic recruiting and managed attrition. However, it must be acknowledged that very few organizations have attained full maturity.

The reasons given for this lack of engagement vary somewhat, but mostly reflect the fact that HR departments simply don't know where to start. There is no apparently clearly defined process. This should not surprise us unduly, because the operational context and actual needs will vary so much. More useful perhaps would be the availability of a range of tools across the maturity levels, from which HR professionals could select what is appropriate for their operational setting. The first stage is to gain an understanding of those levels of forecasting maturity and the key techniques that accompany them. Then we can look at examples of specific tools in action. Figure 2.1 summarizes these levels or approaches.

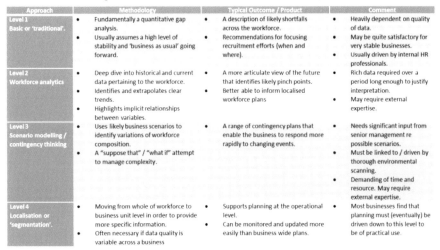

Approach	Methodology	Typical Outcome / Product	Comment
Level 1 **Basic or 'traditional'.**	• Fundamentally a quantitative gap analysis. • Usually assumes a high level of stability and 'business as usual' going forward.	• A description of likely shortfalls across the workforce. • Recommendations for focusing recruitment efforts (when and where).	• Heavily dependent on quality of data. • May be quite satisfactory for very stable businesses. • Usually driven by internal HR professionals.
Level 2 **Workforce analytics**	• Deep dive into historical and current data pertaining to the workforce. • Identifies and extrapolates clear trends. • Highlights implicit relationships between variables.	• A more articulate view of the future that identifies likely pinch points. • Better able to inform localised workforce plans	• Rich data required over a period long enough to justify interpretation. • May require external expertise.
Level 3 **Scenario modelling / contingency thinking**	• Uses likely business scenarios to identify variations of workforce composition. • A "suppose that" / "what if" attempt to manage complexity.	• A range of contingency plans that enable the business to respond more rapidly to changing events.	• Needs significant input from senior management re possible scenarios. • Must be linked to / driven by thorough environmental scanning. • Demanding of time and resource. May require external expertise.
Level 4 **Localisation or 'segmentation'.**	• Moving from whole of workforce to business unit level in order to provide more specific information. • Often necessary if data quality is variable across a business	• Supports planning at the operational level. • Can be monitored and updated more easily than business wide plans.	• Most businesses find that planning must (eventually) be driven down to this level to be of practical use.

Figure 2.1 – Common approaches to forecasting workforce requirement.

Although these levels are shown as distinct, in practice they are cumulative and interdependent. Inevitably, once an organization embraces workforce planning it will evolve methods that may draw from all four approaches.

Forecasting using 'traditional' workforce planning.

This approach can be regarded as the basic 'go to' suite of tools for the HR professional. As with all workforce planning its value is fundamentally dependent on the transparency and clarity of organizational strategy and the quantity and quality of available workforce data. Providing these fundamentals are in place, this basic approach may be all that is required for many organizations. The process steps are as follows:

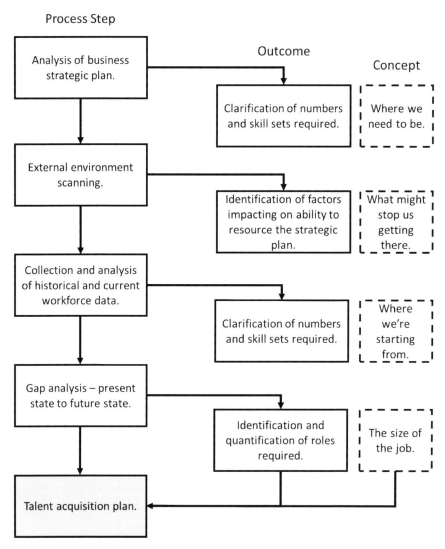

Figure 2.2 – Traditional / basic workforce planning process steps

Augmenting forecasting with workforce analytics.

Most organizations have now come to realize that the traditional approach, rooted in basic headcount data, is a very blunt instrument indeed. The principal catalyst for this shift has undoubtedly been the looming crisis of the ageing workforce. Managing human resource requirement effectively now requires data to be '3-dimensional'; offering greater insights into the nature of workforce issues, as well as their quantum.

Those organizations that have maintained even the most basic human resource information system (HRIS), over a number of years, will have the ability to 'mine' their data and examine the critical relationships between the many variables – if they choose to do so. These interactive and often interdependent variables will include, among others:

- Employee demographics; age profiles, gender, ethnicity etc.
- Turn-over rates.
- Average length of service.
- Average age of retirement.
- Average number of dismissals.
- Average number of deaths in service.
- Average number of medical retirements.
- Recurrent trends in the reason for resignations
- Relative costs e.g. salaried related to retention.
- Job categories most prone to volatility

Examining such data allows the HR professional to see the organization in true relief and to plan to manage workforce risks more effectively. Perhaps the most obvious example here will be the forward plotting of individual ages against the known average age of retirement. This will signal any likely 'spike' periods and enable succession planning to be factored in against the more critical roles. Understanding the costs of recruitment and training will also assist HR and management to consider the benefits of paying higher salaries to improve retention and prevent 'poaching'.

Active and on-going interrogation of these analytics requires some effort, but no great skill in the use of statistics. This is 'plain language' stuff that the majority of HR professionals (perhaps working in collaboration with colleagues in finance) should be able to extract and interpret easily enough. It is more a question of attention to detail than sophisticated technique.

Forecasting for contingency through scenario-modeling.

The VUCA world in which we all now live means that any prediction or forecast cannot be assumed to be self-fulfilling. There is simply too much volatility and uncertainty to allow us to sit back and wait for our view of the future to unfold.

Workforce planning must therefore borrow some of the techniques commonly associated with strategic business planning and risk management. The key questions here are *'what would happen if........?'* and *'suppose that....'* Simple extrapolations from historical data around retirement age or specific role volatility may tell us when and where we are likely to encounter problems, but this is based on an assumed perpetuation of the status quo. Risk management process tell us however, that to assume the status quo and ignore the potential impact of likely scenarios, is to invite disaster. Business planners will routinely be asking questions such as *'how do we respond to the exchange rate at level X, Y or Z?'* and *'what are our alternatives if our current suppliers of critical commodity A gets into trouble?'*. Ultimately safety depends on identifying all the most feasible scenarios and devising strategies to cope with them should they actually occur. Workforce planning, at its best will attempt to do much the same kind of contingency thinking. For example, potential advances in technology and automation should always require us to ask *'do we know of impending changes in plant and process that will in fact make these roles redundant or allow us to work with fewer numbers?'*

Answering questions like these with any degree of confidence requires that HR engages proactively with the business planning process as it unfolds, to ensure that all the pertinent issues are tabled for scrutiny. This is the point at which workforce planning becomes truly strategic.

Section 6 covers scenario modeling in more depth.

Forecasting at localized or segmented levels.

Larger organizations are necessarily more complex. Each component of the workforce will tend to exhibit differentiating characteristics and needs which will eventually call for specific attention. Whole of workforce plans have the merit of indicating general trends, risks and potential solutions, but cannot provide meaningful detailed focus for management interventions.

Organizations will tend to deal with these specific needs in one of three ways:
- 'localizing' the analysis to a specific business unit or department
- 'segmenting' the analysis to particular workforce layers or 'job families'
- Combining the approach by focusing on job families within a business unit or department.

This scaled back approach allows HR analytics to be more acutely focused and may highlight a range of associated issues, such as unacceptable retention rates compared to other comparable departments, inadequate succession planning etc. The more intimate nature of enquiry at this level also allows HR to develop a more informed workforce profile which would include an understanding of motivation and strategies for greater engagement.

Forecasting - all of the above.

In practice, organizations would be well advised to design and adopt a planning process that utilizes all four of the above methods. Despite the now pressing need for fully developed systems many organizations (including their HR departments) continue to procrastinate and offer a litany of reasons for doing so (see page 13). Few HR departments actually manage to engage their senior management teams consistently in the investigation of the most likely or even probable scenarios that should be accounted for. This is a measure of a truly strategic approach to workforce planning and sadly it remains a rare phenomenon.

One thing is certain i.e. the basic 'traditional' approach, used in isolation, will never be sufficient. It must, at the very least, be supported by on-going analysis and interpretation of the environment in which the organization seeks to operate. Our VUCA world demands this absolutely. Consequently the practice of environmental scanning must be accepted as a critical routine for HR departments as an essential element of their business partnering.

References.

1. For a full discussion see:
   http://www.innovationaus.com/2015/08/STEM-vs-STEAM

2. ManpowerGroup. 2015. *Talent Shortage Survey.* Available at: *http://www.manpowergroup.com/wps/wcm/connect/db23c560-08b6-485f-9bf6-5f38a43c76a/2015_Talent_Shortage_Survey_US-lo_res.pdf?MOD=AJPERES*

3. Laurano, M. 2009. *The Modern Approach to Workforce Planning.* Bersin and Associates Research Report. Page 12

3

Environmental scanning – a critical routine to support strategy.

Environmental scanning – the macro perspective.

All organizations (especially those who are engaged in competitive markets) should engage in on-going analysis of the specific worlds in which they must operate. The peculiar combinations of these worlds creates an operational environment ultimately unique to each entity, but to some extent shared with others e.g. customers, competitors, stakeholders etc. A comprehensive understanding of the operational environment will enable an organization to optimize opportunities and to minimize risk or threats. A useful definition is provided by Kroon (1995):

Environmental scanning can be defined as the study and interpretation of the political, economic, social and technological events and trends which influence a business, an industry or even a total market. (1)

This definition refers to the external environment and a globalized perspective. Consequently it can be thought of as *macro-scanning*. The concept of macro-scanning directs us toward the most commonly used tool for environmental scanning i.e. PEST analysis (political, economic, social and technological). Most organizations today would however, find PEST to be a rather 'stripped down' view of the world. Consequently a number of variants have come into being to meet specific organizational needs. The actual variant initially selected by an organization may itself need to be reviewed as circumstances change.

Basic PEST criteria.

Creation of the basic PEST analysis is usually credited to Harvard professor Francis Aguilar. His original tool was presented in his 1967 book, *Scanning the Business Environment* (2). The root criteria were originally cited as ETPS but were inevitably rearranged into the more memorable PEST – political, economic, social and technological factors. The depth to which each of these criteria are explored will depend on organizational needs, expertise and resources. While each criterion could be more or less infinitely expanded, there are certain core considerations which should never be ignored.

P - Political considerations.

With smaller organizations operating within their national boundaries, discussion of potential political impacts may be limited to the domestic landscape. However, once a business begins to operate beyond its original national borders, either through importing or exports, the political implications become significantly more complex. The key factors to consider are:

- Do we understand the true nature of the political system in which we are operating, or intend to operate?
- How stable is that political system? Would any change of government bring about significant shifts in how businesses are allowed to operate?
- Who is currently in power? Do we really understand their view of the world? Is that perspective sympathetic to our operations – or at least tolerant?

- What specific views does the current government hold in regard to key operating conditions e.g.
  - Taxation regimes
  - Property rights
  - Employment law
  - Health & safety legislation
  - Customer rights
  - Corporate social responsibility etc.
- Is there evidence of corrupt practice in dealings with government bodies or officials?
- What do we know of any impending legislative changes? Could they significantly impact the way we do business?
- Who could potentially replace the current government? How do their views differ from the incumbents?
- Are our export markets particularly subject to terrorism or revolutionary activity? How would we guard against these risks?
- Are we subject to multi-lateral or bi-lateral trade or operating agreements e.g.
  - General agreement on tariffs and trade (GATT)
  - General agreement on trade in services
  - Central European free trade agreement
  - Trans Pacific Partnership (TPP)
  - European free trade arrangements

  If so, what constraints do they impose, what opportunities do they offer?

E – Economic considerations.

Again, there will be local and global issues to be considered here e.g.

- Where are we (internally and externally) in the economic cycle – growth, recession, stagnation? What are the implications for the spending power of our customers etc.?

- What is the exchange rate situation for the currencies we deal in when exporting or importing? How are these rates tracking against our projections?
- What is the state of the labour market? A tightening market may drive up the costs of maintaining a skilled workforce.
- To what extent are our products dependent on disposable income? Are incomes being affected by headwinds such as increasing mortgage rates, inflation etc.
- Are any of our key production costs likely to increase significantly i.e. beyond projections.
- What are the prevailing conditions around access to credit – for us and for our customers? Are these likely to change? If, so in what way and how would this impact us?
- Are there other emerging costs that we need to account for e.g. increasing compliance requirements, unforeseen commodity / materials shortages etc.

S – social-cultural considerations.

Perhaps the most complex of these core considerations, societal change is always difficult to grasp, largely due to its often subliminal nature. Many of the shifts that occur go unnoticed until they emerge into mainstream culture, and this can put organizations into a reactive mode. Social change is also shaped significantly by the other core factors; economics, politics and perhaps most significantly by technological advances. For some businesses, for example manufacturers of paving slabs, social change is of little interest, but for mobile phone manufacturers, it is a critical concern because they are dependent on the shifts in consumer tastes. For these businesses it is imperative not only to understand the shifts that occur in both local and global societies but perhaps to attempt to shape them? Indeed, some companies are so successful in dictating to their customers what they simply must go out and buy that they create their own brand of 'fashion victim'.

Key considerations in this area are:

- Demographics – are we fully aware of the trends in population growth rates and age profiles in each of the countries in which we operate? How will these trends affect our product / service design or relevance? For example, manufacturers of traditional wrist watches will face falling demand for their products in countries with an increasing proportion of younger people – this function is built into their mobile devices.
- Education – is the education system of our workforce supplier countries producing people with the skills we need in the kinds of quantities we need?
- How pronounced are the supposed differences of mind-set between the various generations in our workforces and in our customer base?
- Do we have to deal with issues arising from a multi-generational workforce?
- Do we have strategies for dealing with the actual or potential aging workforce i.e. the retirement of the baby boomers?
- Are we fully aware of the cultural and religious influences at work in our export markets?
- To what extent, if any, are different languages impeding our business operations.

T – technological considerations.

Technological advance is most certainly the fastest moving of the business environment factors – so much so that no single organization could justifiably claim to be fully abreast of what is happening around us. This may be the reality, but every organization that wishes to optimize its operations (especially in the face of competition) must join the race to 'keep in the game'. As J.G. Ballard reminds us:

Science and technology multiply around us. To an increasing extent they dictate the languages in which we speak and think. Either we use those languages, or we remain mute. (3)

The key factors for consideration are:

- Are we monitoring the technological environment well enough to be confident that we have not missed out on innovations or worthwhile upgrades?
- Do we know what technical / technological advances our competitors are pursuing or have recently made?
- Are we aware of what new skills our people may need if we move to a new technology?
- Are we optimizing technology to reduce costs e.g. reducing travel and accommodation costs through teleconferencing, on-line training etc.?
- Are we sufficiently active in R&D, either as stand-alone or a joint venture initiative?

Variants of the PEST model.

Each organization should analyze its operating model and develop the PEST variant that captures the full range of potential impacts on its own operations. The most common variants are:

SLEPT: Socio-cultural, Legal, Economic, Political and Technological. The addition here is the consideration of the legislative environment and would encompass everything from requirements for financial reporting through to health and safety compliance. Most sizeable organizations will employ, or have ready access to legal counsel to ensure that their operations remain within legally prescribed boundaries and to interpret the effects of new legislation for senior management.

PESTEL: Political, Economic, Socio-cultural, Technological, Environmental, Legal. Here we see the addition of the environmental factor. Care for the environment has become a major issue in the minds of the general public and consequently in the manifestos of the political parties. Most organizations now realize that demonstrating environmental responsibility is not simply a matter of compliance, it is essential for positive 'branding' and ultimately for customer support. Many companies now make environmental concern the flag-bearer of their identity. They inhabit what Price Waterhouse Coopers analysts call the 'Green World'. These organizations champion themselves as:

Companies which care, in which social responsibility dominates the corporate agenda with concerns about changes in climate and demographics, and embedding sustainability becomes becoming the key drivers of business. (4)

STEEPLE: Socio-cultural, Technological, Economic, Environmental, Political, Legal. Ethical. Here we see another 'green world' influence emerging i.e. ethics. Obviously linked to environmental concerns, but also considering the human condition, businesses now need to demonstrate a concern for the well-being of their workforces and of course of their customers. It is no longer acceptable to set up 'sweat shops' in the third world and exploit them ruthlessly in search of maximum profit. Neither is acceptable to cut costs to the bone by giving the customer an inferior or potentially dangerous product.

PESTLIED: Political, Economic, Socio-cultural, Technological, Legal, Information, Environmental, Demographic. This variant takes quite a different perspective with the addition of two specific criteria; information and demographic. This would be especially applicable to organizations whose core operations revolve around the acquisition of information or business intelligence and who need to understand the impact of the various generations and mobility on the market place.

Marketing specialists, for example, would benefit from this particular model.

LONGPESTEL: This variant adds the dimensions of Local, National and Global considerations to the PESTEL variant. It is especially useful for multi-national organizations that need to understand how specific concerns will impact across the various theatres of their operations.

Conducting a PEST analysis (or alternative variant).

Self-evidently, attempting a PEST analysis as an individual working alone, is likely to be of limited value when compared to a 'meeting of minds'. Managing the contributions of a group can however be a difficult undertaking, especially if the group members are not familiar with the concepts involved and have come to the process 'cold'. Face to face meetings are expensive and the time available must therefore be maximized.

To maximize the value of the face to face group session it is advisable to appoint a skilled facilitator who can guide the process and stimulate thinking with numerous examples. If possible, the facilitator should 'prime the pump' by engaging the group members in initial thinking ahead of the face to face session. This can be achieved through a distance version of the nominal group technique (5). Using electronic communication, the facilitator provides each member of the group with a brief explanation of the PEST variant process and what is meant by each criterion. In addition, a template is provided into which the individual is asked to insert his / her initial thoughts around each of the criteria. Several days at least should be allowed for this. The facilitator then collates the returns into a master template for 'start up' at the face to face session. This process ensures that group members arrive with 'runs on the board' and are already involved in the process. Furthermore, and crucially, it ensures that the opinions of less vocal members are captured, at least at the outset.

After collating the returns, the facilitator should attempt independent research around the opinions expressed in order to bring more substance to the face-to-face discussion. At the meeting he / she then opens up a more focused re-examination of the criteria and notes the key points arising. Having a skilled typist on hand to enter findings directly into the template displayed on screen will allow the facilitator to concentrate on opening up and provoking quality discussion. The facilitator must also take care to direct group members' attention to what is likely to happen (future focus) as well as considering what is currently happening.

When discussion is more or less exhausted, the meeting can be closed and the facilitator undertakes to circulate the completed template for final consideration before moving to the next stage.

Where to from here – SWOT analysis.

The PEST variant analysis is essentially a scanning tool. It will produce a great deal of relatively incoherent information which is of little use until interpreted for its potential impact on the organization. The information needs to be vigorously interrogated to bring it into three dimensions. A much-favoured method for adding the dimension of meaning is the SWOT analysis.

Although a familiar feature in most management environments, the origins of the technique remain obscure. The standard method involves the use of a grid template (see figure 3.1 below) but users should be aware of the subliminal suggestion that sufficient thinking has been done once the boxes are filled. Boxes may in fact equate to constrained thinking. It may be preferable to abandon the grid and work on separate sheets e.g. using flip charts and work the categories through to natural exhaustion. It is good practice, if possible, to re-run SWOT sessions over a short period. Invariably additional ideas will occur to individuals in the intervening period and these often prove to be significant.

S (Strengths)	**W** (Weaknesses)
Is the organization / business in a position of relative strength in relation to the issues identified. List the issues here and any qualifying observations / supporting information.	Is the organization / business particularly exposed to unacceptable risk or lacking in required resources in relation to the issues identified. List the issues here and any qualifying observations / supporting information.
O (Opportunities)	**T** (Threats)
Which of the issues identifies represents potential opportunities for the business / organisation e.g. gaps in the market, the demise of a competitor, new technology etc. List the issues here and any qualifying observations / supporting information.	Which of the issues identifies poses an actual or potential threat for the business / organisation e.g. new competitors emerging, unpredictable FX, changes of government overseas etc. List the issues here and any qualifying observations / supporting information.

Figure 3.1 – SWOT analysis: the standard grid.

SWOT to So What?

Once again SWOT as a tool needs further work if its findings are to be of real value. Each of the strengths, weaknesses, opportunities and threats identified needs to be interrogated by the simple challenge – "So what?" *So what* does this actually mean for us? *So what* do we need to do to mitigate this risk? *So what* do we need to do to take advantage of this situation?" etc. It is easy to see how this interrogation starts to inform strategic planning and the formulation of objectives.

Environmental scanning – the micro-perspective.

In addition to lifting their heads up to scan the global horizon, businesses will also need to focus in on their immediate core operations and on-going sustainability. SWOT will do this to a degree, but is often regarded as too broad to generate tightly-focused micro information on the current forces impacting business performance.

A tool commonly used to produce this kind of micro analysis is Porter's five forces illustrated below at figure 3.2.

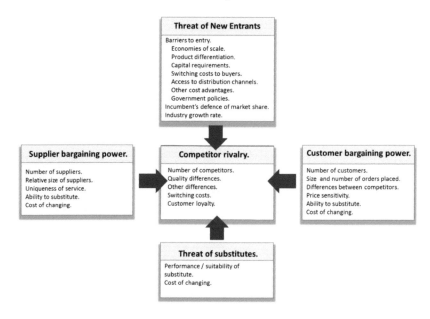

Figure 3.2 – Porter's Five Forces analysis.

It is immediately obvious that Porter's model is based on the principle that businesses exist in a state of competition with each other and that they are continually required to respond to threats and pressures (6). While this undoubtedly true in a general sense, it is not always applicable e.g. when businesses enter into partnerships or alliances. The model often attracts criticism for being difficult to apply to dynamic markets and for overlooking what are now regarded as critical factors. For example, when considering competitors, Porter does not consider their access to either intellectual or human capital. In the context of workforce planning this is a serious omission. As the baby boomers retire in droves, replaced, in the developed world, by a significantly smaller Generation X, businesses are having to compete as never before for staff in a diminishing talent pool. Nevertheless, providing these additional concerns are adequately included, the model offers a useful method for determining where the business sits in the current specific environment.

Teasing out the people issues.

The purpose of environmental scanning, macro and micro, is of course to inform the processes of strategic business planning. Emergent business plans tend to focus directly on what is to be achieved, and (traditionally at least) rarely on who is to achieve it. This is particularly true of businesses that undergo relatively little change and have historically low staff turnovers. But even these must now face up, potentially, to both quantitative and qualitative staffing issues. Consequently, as strategic objectives are formulated, senior managers need to interrogate them to reveal any potential people issues and action plan for their resolution.

Figure 3.3 below schematizes the key questions we need to consider when teasing out the people issues arising from the business planning process. This is bound to be a dynamic process e.g. as people are recruited the analysis will need to be updated and refreshed.

Although at first sight this kind of analysis looks like a specifically HR function, it cannot be effectively achieved without the input of a number of key stakeholders, particularly in the area of succession planning. We are probably entitled to expect an HR team to possess the skills needed to use the typical tools and processes, but this is not always the case and external expertise may be required. Furthermore, a number of the tools are dependent on access to quality historical HR data.

The following sections will examine these key questions in more depth and describe typical tools used to provide adequate answers to them.

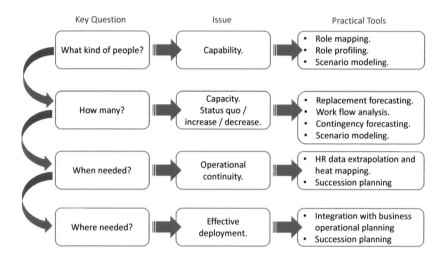

Figure 3.3 – Identifying the people issues.

In section 4 we will specifically address the issues of *capability*. In simple terms this refers to the knowledge, skills and aptitudes an individual requires to perform well in a role. Increasingly, capability also accounts for quality of experience and, given increasing shortages of skilled people, a perception of an individual's potential to learn and grow into a role.

References.

1. Kroon, J. (1995). *General Management*. Pearson, South Africa. Page 76.
2. Aguilar, F. (1967). *Scanning the Buisiness Environment*. MacMillan. New York.

3. Ballard, J.G. (1995). Introduction to *Crash*. Vintage Books.

4. Price Waterhouse Cooper (2014). *The future of work – a journey to 2022*. Available at: *http://www.pwc.com/gx/en/issues/talent/future-of-work/journey-to-2022.html*

5. See Delbecq, A.L. and VandeVen, A.H. (1971). *A Group Process Model for Problem Identification and Programe Planning*. Journal of Applied Science. Vol 7. Pp 466-91

   See Porter, M.E. (1980). *Competitive Strategy*. Free Press. New York

4

Capability issues – what kind of people?

Defining role capability – role mapping.

The purpose of the basic role map is to provide a detailed specification of what the incumbent is expected to do (role functions) in a specific role, in a specific organization, at a specific time. In that sense they are unique and do not transfer *holus bolus* to other organizations. They are therefore fundamentally different from generic competency frameworks which will be discussed later. Carroll & Boutall (2011) define the purpose of functional analysis as follows:

Functional analysis is the main tool we use to define the nature of an occupational sector and the functions performed within it. This is an essential process in defining occupational competence and in setting boundaries between different occupations. Without a functional map we would not be able to say where one occupational area ends and another begins. (2)

A role map should also describe the *relative importance* of the required functions (criticality). Fully developed maps may go on to identify other requirements such as enabling skills and aptitudes. These are extremely useful for recruiting or promoting into the role. Function description will not suffice on its own to fully encompass a role, but it is without doubt the most important aspect. After all, the first thing we want to understand when we move to a new role is "what exactly do I have to do?"

Mapping roles is a time-consuming process and requires a level of expertise that can prove costly where it is not available internally. Consequently, very few organizations are comprehensively mapped. However, those that are fully mapped are much better placed to drive key management and HR processes.

There is no standard format or template for a role map, but due to the common sense logic involved, the variants are inevitably very similar. Similarly, the terminology may vary according to organizational preference, but the process invariably involves a 'drilling down' through layers of functionality. For present purposes I shall use the following terms to indicate the layers of analysis:

- Role purpose
- Primary function
- Associated task
- Associated activity

Figure 4.1 below illustrates these concepts as a drill down hierarchy.

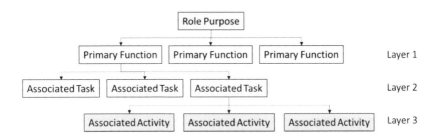

Figure 4.1 – The 'Drill Down' layers of functional analysis.

All functional role maps will drill down to layer 2. Going deeper will necessarily involve a good deal of work and organizations must ask themselves whether they need that degree of detail. It should be understood that this level of analysis is only justifiable for roles that change only incrementally and are fairly predictable in terms of performance.

The mapping process first identifies the primary functions associated with the role. These are simple, high level descriptors, generally few in number and are perhaps best thought of as the basic skeleton or framework of the role upon which all the detail is suspended. For example, if we look at the role of a shift manager in a manufacturing environment we might identify the following:

Figure 4.2 – Example of Primary Functions

These primary functions would not of course be standard for all shift managers in all contexts. Their identification results from discussion with line managers and other key stakeholders.

In this example, the shift manager role is essentially that of a front line supervisor whose performance is largely iterative and predictable.

Consequently his / her role can be broken down and closely articulated. The next stage is to take each primary function and open it up to reveal layer 2 functionality. Once again this will require close consultation with relevant managers by the mapping facilitator. Functional maps of this kind are often accused of reflecting the 'status quo' but the facilitator can easily add a future focus (relative to the organization's strategic plan) by asking not just 'what do they do?' but also 'what will you need them to do in the future?'

Figure 4.3 below shows layer 2 being opened up for the shift manager example. In this case, consultation with managers revealed that the standard tasks routinely carried out could be defined satisfactorily via the classic POSDCORB management model i.e. planning, organizing, staffing, directing, coordinating, reporting and budgeting. This model thus provided a 'screen' through which the primary functions could be filtered to reveal the specific activities associated with those tasks i.e. layer 3.

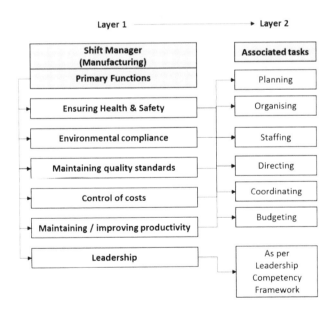

Figure 4.3 – Example of functional analysis to layer 2

The leadership function is treated separately because it is unlikely to be iterative. The task level here is related to a specific competency framework which will provide the appropriate level of behavioural description.

Figure 4.4 below illustrates how drilling down to layer 3 occurs.

	Layer 1	Layer 2	Layer 3
Role Ref.	Primary Function	Associated Tasks	Associated Activities
1.	Health and Safety (H&S)	1.1 - Planning	1.1.1 – Scheduling regular H&S meetings. 1.1.2 – Ensuring that new staff receive H&S inductions at the earliest opportunity following arrival on site. 1.1.3 – Ensuring that all H&S critical routines are adhered to e.g. inspections, hazard ID, emergency drills etc. 1.1.4 – Action planning for unforeseen safety issues e.g. isolations, confined space working etc. 1.1.5 – Carrying out risk assessments for and mitigation planning for situational H&S issues as required.
		1.2 - Organising	1.2.1 – Ensuring that all requirements for H&S meetings are met e.g. venue, attendee notification / invitation, equipment, agenda etc. 1.2.2 – Ensuring that all requirements for emergency drills are adhered to as per relevant SOP's. 1.2.3 – Ensuring induction requirements are met for all new staff e.g. PPE issue, training etc. 1.2.4 – Ensuring that isolation plans are effectively implemented. 1.2.5 – Ensuring that Fit4Work compliance is implemented. 1.2.6 – Ensuring that Safe Behaviour Observations (SBO's) are effectively carried out as per shift cycle planning – both those allocated to shift personnel and to self.
		1.3 - Staffing	1.3.1 – Ensuring all shift personnel are competent in all required safety related knowledge and skills e.g. isolations, confined space working, emergency procedures etc. 1.3.2 – Effectively managing call-outs to cover short term absence due to sickness or previously authorised activity. 1.3.3 – Ensuring adequate cover is arranged for long term injury or sickness. 1.3.4 – Following up any injury to shift personnel to ensure appropriate treatment is put in place and monitoring subsequent progress to recovery. 1.3.5 – Participating in or contributing, as required, to long term

Figure 4.4 – Example functional analysis (extract) to layer 3

A good deal of rigorous process is needed here to ask for each of the primary functions in turn "what planning, organizing, staffing, directing, coordinating or budgeting activities are undertaken?" The extract shows the health and safety function being opened up. It is easy to see that analysis of this sort may result in a substantial document and some organizations may question its value due to the initial investment of time and skilled resource. However, once completed, the role map provides absolute clarity of expectations for the role incumbent, for the manager, for recruitment, for learning and development activity, for performance management and for identifying the inter-relationship with other roles. This much said, it must be admitted that functional analysis to this depth may not be practical for fast-moving industries where roles are constantly being re-shaped.

The information revealed at figure 4.4, while undoubtedly valuable, remains 'two dimensional' because neither the role incumbent nor the manager is informed of which tasks are more critical than others. We need to describe relative performance needs. This can be done through the use of performance categories.

Performance categories.

Each occupational role function is rated (generally by agreement between manager and role incumbent) to determine its relative criticality. The system used here derives from the U.S. Department of Labour analysis which provides for 3 levels of performance criticality. These are:

- **Mastery** – this indicates the highest level of competence. The need here is for 100% familiarity and compliance to standard. The individual should never need to refer to others for assistance or advice. These competencies reflect the essential nature of the job and should provide the backbone of performance recruitment, development and performance management.
- **High Conformity** – this indicates a high level of competence. However, the need here is not absolutely critical, allowing the individual some scope and time to adjust performance, or, if necessary, to consult or take advice on matters of detail etc.
- **Low Conformity** – this indicates a relatively low level of required competence. Essentially this refers to background knowledge, peripheral skills or additional expertise that indi-

viduals may develop. These competencies do not impact on the critical aspect of operations or service delivery.

Categorizing role functions in this way provides a meaningful 'profile' that reveals what is really important, and sifts out the less significant aspects that can detract from overall clarity.

Figure 4.5 below shows the performance categories being added to each specific associated activity in the role map, designated by M (mastery), HC (high conformity) and LC (low conformity).

Role Ref.	Primary Function	Associated Tasks	Associated Activities	Performance Category		
				M	HC	LC
1.	Health and Safety (H&S)	1.1 - Planning	1.1.1 – Scheduling regular H&S meetings.		X	
			1.1.2 – Ensuring that new staff receive H&S inductions at the earliest opportunity following arrival on site.	X		
			1.1.3 – Ensuring that all H&S critical routines are adhered to e.g. inspections, hazard ID, emergency drills etc.	X		
			1.1.4 – Action planning for unforeseen safety issues e.g. isolations, confined space working etc.		X	
			1.1.5 – Carrying out risk assessments for and mitigation planning for situational H&S issues as required.		X	
		1.2 - Organising	1.2.1 – Ensuring that all requirements for H&S meetings are met e.g. venue, attendee notification / invitation, equipment, agenda etc.		X	
			1.2.2 – Ensuring that all requirements for emergency drills are adhered to as per relevant SOP's.		X	
			1.2.3 – Ensuring induction requirements are met for all new staff e.g. PPE issue, training etc.	X		
			1.2.4 – Ensuring that isolation plans are effectively implemented.	X		
			1.2.5 – Ensuring that Fit4Work compliance is implemented.		X	
			1.2.6 – Ensuring that Safe Behaviour Observations (SBO's) are effectively carried out as per shift cycle planning – both those allocated to shift personnel and to self.		X	
		1.3 - Staffing	1.3.1 – Ensuring all shift personnel are competent in all required safety related knowledge and skills e.g. isolations, confined space working, emergency procedures etc.		X	
			1.3.2 – Effectively managing call-outs to cover short term absence due to sickness or previously authorised activity.		X	
			1.3.3 – Ensuring adequate cover is arranged for long term injury or sickness.		X	
			1.3.4 – Following up any injury to shift personnel to ensure appropriate treatment is put in place and monitoring subsequent progress to recovery.		X	
			1.3.5 – Participating in or contributing, as required, to long term			

Figure 4.5 – Example functional analysis (extract) including performance categories.

It is important that all those contributing to functional analysis of this kind have a mutual understanding of what is meant by each of the performance categories. Role incumbents will tend to regard everything they do as mastery – but this is never true. The role of the facilitator is key to maintaining appropriate perspectives.

Defining capability – role profiling.

As noted, functional analysis by role mapping is well suited to stable, routine, iterative performance. It is less suited (perhaps entirely so), to roles that are subject to significant levels of unpredictability or which require more abstract skills. Management and leadership roles are obvious examples due to the varying degrees of proactive and reactive commitment required and the range of 'soft skills' needed. Less obvious perhaps are technical roles such as we find in engineering. While these are rooted in 'hard skills' the manner in which those skills are called upon is often unpredictable.

With roles of this sort it may be advisable to define functionality through a *role profile.* The role map approach defines what the incumbent will certainly be called on to do *as a matter of routine.* The role profile attempts to define the knowledge, skills and attributes an individual should possess in order to be confident that she can meet functional requirements *as they arise*. In this sense, a role profile is *situationally driven*. We could usefully think of the role profile as the 'toolbox' the individual needs in order to adapt to differing problems and contexts. For example, a manager moving to a new organization may find that the new job needs to address significantly different issues and thus requires a different combination of tools. Trying to define functional requirements for every conceivable situation would inevitably prove futile.

Clearly, the task of identifying and describing the full 'tool box' can be daunting, depending on the complexity of the role. To do this from scratch would entail the use of a number of techniques such as long term on the job observation, log books, operational debriefs etc. Fortunately this work has been done for us across numerous roles by organizations such as the ILO (International Labour Organisation) (3) the Canadian Job Bank (4) and O-Net online (5).

The classification system varies somewhat between these international archives and the researcher must eventually choose that which suits his organization best. As an example O-Net uses the following inventory to build a role profile:

- Tasks potentially carried out
- Tools and Technology used
- Knowledge requirements
- Skills
- Abilities
- Work activities
- Work context
- Job zone
- Educational expectations (qualifications)

So, thus far we have acquired a detailed view of what the role incumbent is required to do, but we have no definition of the relative criticality of these functions i.e. which ones are the most important. This issue is central to the design of training and of performance management systems because we need to be sure that we are focusing on the right things. We deal with this by working with managers, and those experienced in the role, to categorize each function as either *mastery, high conformity* or *low conformity* in terms of performance. Essentially this process shifts the analysis from 2 dimensions to a 3 dimensional landscape. For newly emerging and future roles much of this performance analysis will be based on intelligent projection from past experience of similar roles. Once a role is established a review would be needed to confirm initial thinking.

While resources such as these are hugely valuable, the information obtained remains somewhat 2-dimensional, once again, in that we are offered no guidance as to which factors are most significant. This is hardly surprising given that the precise functionality of a specific role will vary according to the workplace requirement. The job of teasing out relative performance criticalities must fall to local expertise. The simplest way to approach this is to assemble the raw profile information (from a source such as O-Net) and then align it to a rating system for local managers, technical experts etc. to consider.

Various types of rating can be applied. If, for example, we build a profile for a chemical / process engineer we will need to consider relative importance in terms of how much time is spent (on average) on the main tasks and in terms of the relative importance of the skills required to perform those tasks. Figure 4.6 refers shows the identified main tasks being assessed as a proportion of workload.

Main Tasks	Av.% of workload
Evaluate chemical equipment and processes to identify ways to optimize performance or to ensure compliance with safety and environmental regulations	30
Conduct research to develop new and improved chemical manufacturing processes.	5
Design and plan layout of equipment.	15
Determine most effective arrangement of operations such as mixing, crushing, heat transfer, distillation, and drying.	5
Develop processes to separate components of liquids or gases or generate electrical currents using controlled chemical processes	0
Develop safety procedures to be employed by workers operating equipment or working in close proximity to on-going chemical reactions.	3
Perform laboratory studies of steps in manufacture of new product and test proposed process in small scale operation such as a pilot plant.	5
Troubleshoot problems with chemical manufacturing processes.	10
Design measurement and control systems for chemical plants based on data collected in laboratory experiments and in pilot plant operations.	7
Direct activities of workers who operate or who are engaged in constructing and improving absorption, evaporation, or electromagnetic equipment.	5
Prepare estimate of production costs and production progress reports for management.	5
Perform tests and monitor performance of processes throughout stages of production to determine degree of control over variables such as temperature, density, specific gravity, and pressure.	10
Total	100

Figure 4.6 – Example of main task workload rating.

Other factors such as knowledge, skills, experience etc. could be rated using a simple Likert scale as shown in the extract at Figure 4.7 below.

Naturally, it is important for the profile builder to consult as widely as possible among those 'qualified' to comment in order to obtain a comprehensive and balanced view of the role in context. Ratings can be averaged across the respondent group and any significant variants resolved through discussion.

Skills	Rating				
	1	2	3	4	5
Science - Using scientific rules and methods to solve problems.					X
Critical Thinking - Using logic and reasoning to identify the strengths and weaknesses of alternative solutions, conclusions or approaches to problems.				X	
Complex Problem Solving - Identifying complex problems and reviewing related information to develop and evaluate options and implement solutions.					X
Judgment and Decision Making - Considering the relative costs and benefits of potential actions to choose the most appropriate one.			X		
Systems Analysis - Determining how a system should work and how changes in conditions, operations, and the environment will affect outcomes.				X	
Mathematics - Using mathematics to solve problems.			X		
Reading Comprehension - Understanding written sentences and paragraphs in work related documents.					X
Active Learning - Understanding the implications of new information for both current and future problem-solving and decision-making.				X	
Systems Evaluation - Identifying measures or indicators of system performance and the actions needed to improve or correct performance, relative to the goals of the system.				X	
Speaking - Talking to others to convey information effectively.			X		
Operations Analysis - Analysing needs and product requirements to create a design.		X			

Figure 4.7 – Example of skills criticality rating (extract)

Monitoring and expanding existing capability.

Capability has a number of dimensions; individual, team and organizational. Thus far we have focused on individual capability but to be strategically effective managers should be more concerned by overall *team* capability. Mitigating risks to operational continuity and optimizing the ability to respond to workplace challenges depends, ultimately, on the flexibility of the team. Teams that are rooted in a culture of permanently fixed roles, based on single skill-sets are hardly teams at all. They are not able to support each other when things get tough.

The task of workforce planning in this respect comes down to a thorough understanding of where team skill levels sit and actively planning to maximize capability potential through up-skilling and cross-skilling. Naturally, this is easier to achieve with lower level, less complex roles, but much can be achieved with higher level roles if managers are prepared to engage with tactics such as role shadowing and rotation.

The team skills matrix.

An essential tool for managing team capability is the *team skills matrix*. It is ideally suited to operational levels e.g. production or service delivery teams but the principles can be applied to higher level functions.

Figure 4.8 below shows a typical matrix, in this example for team of airport security officers. In this context we need to understand that the team manager must confront the need to maintain vigilance and alertness as well as expertise. Allowing team members to become locked into one specific function could, potentially, encourage boredom and complacency.

In this example, role mapping has revealed the functional requirements of the aircraft guarding role, together with the various performance categories i.e. mastery, high conformity or low conformity. The matrix uses a simple 1-5 rating scale with a rating of 3 set as the minimum operational standard. Those performing below this pose a degree of risk that must be mitigated through development or performance management. The matrix reveals the 3-dimensional nature of team skills and allows the manager to strategize for incremental improvement of capability across the board. We can see that officers E, F and H fall below the minimum standard. There may be rational explanations for this e.g. they may be new starters – but they pose unacceptable risks and the shortfall must be addressed. Tools of this kind also help the task of deployment planning. For example we would not want to see officers E, F or H on duty without more experienced officers present. Officer A is clearly the most accomplished and careful consideration should be given as to how he should be used e.g. as a coach or mentor. He might also be a flight risk if the role offers insufficient challenge.

Team Skills Matrix - Ref (Aircraft Guard Duties)										
Number of skills =		8 (enter number)								

	Current Skill Specific Ratings									
	Skill 1	Skill 2	Skill 3	Skill 4	Skill 5	Skill 6	Skill 7	Skill 8		
	Performance Category i.e.Mastery, High Conformity, Low Conformity									
Staff Member	HC	M	M	M	HC	M	M	HC	Total	Current Aggregate
Officer A	5	5	5	5	5	5	5	5	40	5
Officer B	4	4	4	3	4	4	4	4	31	3.875
Officer C	5	4	4	4	4	4	5	4	34	4.25
Officer D	4	5	4	4	4	4	4	4	33	4.125
Officer E	3	3	3	3	3	3	3	3	24	3
Officer F	2	2	2	1	3	2	2	2	16	2
Officer G	5	5	4	4	5	3	4	5	35	4.375
Officer H	1	2	2	2	1	3	2	2	15	1.875
	29	30	28	26	29	28	29	29		
									Team Perf Av.	3.5625

Rating Descriptors	5=	Expert standard. Can be used to train others in this skill.	
	4=	Highly competent. Can be left to supervise others in this area.	
	3=	Competent - at the minimum required standard.	*Organisational Minimum Standard
	2=	Improving - but remains under the minmum standard.	
	1=	Very weak. Needs constant supervision.	
	0=	Has no discernible ability in this area whatsoever.	

Skill Descriptions	1=	Radio Communication with Sergeant and Operations
	2=	Notify Operations when aircraft on blocks and push back.
	3=	Check IDs of people entering the cabin
	4=	Wand people every time they enter the cabin to procedure standard.
	5=	Notify the aircraft search team of the progress of the cleaners on board
	6=	Wand and check the cleaners and caterers prior to them entering the aircraft.
	7=	Notify engineers if any problems found during aircraft screening .
	8=	Public relations with airline staff and passengers.

Figure 4.8 – Simple team skills matrix.

Ratings will be determined by performance in training, observations and delivery of required outcomes. In some situations these matrices are use publicly but in most cases operate as a 'behind the scenes' management tool.

Figure 4.8 reflects the performance of just one team but by using the team performance average managers can directly compare with other teams. For example, in the context of airport security, shifts can be compared, either at a specific airport, or across all the airports at which the organization functions. This is powerful information when planning for capability improvement. Using this data, useful strategies become available, such as moving personnel between shifts, or perhaps even locations, to even out and hopefully improve performance.

Clearly, this approach becomes increasingly difficult with higher level, roles that are more fluid and less predictable in terms of required performance e.g. management, technical specialists etc. Capability for roles of this sort may place as much reliance on how responsibilities are discharged as it does on specific skills and knowledge i.e. on *how* the individual goes about her work as well as *what* she actually does. This takes us into the realm of behavioural analysis as an indicator of required capability.

Behavioural analysis.

In its most basic form, identification of the required or desired behaviours for success in a given role may be no more than a 'wish list' of aptitudes or personality traits. The 'big five' personality test or OCEAN model (6) is an example of such low level thinking. Above this are numerous other psychometric tools that allow an insight into personality and how an individual is likely to behave, over time. The most prominent among these are probably the Myers Briggs Personality Test (MBTI), 16 PF, The Eysenck Personality Questionnaire, DISC Assessment and the True Colours Test. Such tests may provide valuable information when considering whether an individual is the 'right fit' in terms of the overall balance of a team. They are less useful when it comes to assessing whether or not somebody is likely to perform well in a given role. If we are not careful we can be led into harmful generalizations e.g. the frequently heard assertions that introverted characters are unsuited to leadership roles or extraverted individuals are poor finishers.

Each of us, as individuals, brings a personality mix to the table. We also bring experiences which have, in most cases, allowed us to adapt to our workplace environment sufficiently well to perform adequately – in some cases exceptionally. It is this constant adaptation that broadens our skills and ultimately makes us more 'valuable' to employers. However, adapting and performing well will only be possible if the individual has a very clear view of what is expected. We have seen that role mapping can identify the functional requirements. Depending on functional analysis alone can lead to a 'micro' view of the world and the danger of failing to see the bigger picture. Role functions need to be discharged within a set of specified behaviours that align the individual holistically with organizational values and standards. This is the world of *competencies.*

There appears to be no universally agreed definition of what a competency is but there is emerging consensus around the concepts promoted by David McClelland, who is generally regarded as the father of the modern competency movement.

As McClelland showed, it is necessary to look beyond the basic skills and knowledge required to perform an adequate job into the deeply rooted competencies – an individual's social role, self-image, traits, and motives – that can most accurately determine high-potential candidates. In addition, an individual's competencies must fit, or be able to fit through development, those required to achieve outstanding performance in the job. (7)

This observation points to the work that organizations must do if they are to achieve the optimum employee-to-role alignment. They must bring together functional analysis, aptitudes, ideal personality attributes and patterns of conduct in a holistically descriptive form – the modern competency description. McClelland's *Iceberg Model* (8) tells us that much of an individual's overall competence is *subliminal* i.e. lies beneath the surface and is not easily discernible.

McClelland's view was that organizations must first define for themselves the competencies that are acceptable for somebody to start work in a role. These are now commonly referred to as the *threshold* competencies. Secondly, they should attempt to define additional competencies or higher levels of performance that would characterize outstanding performance. These are known as the *differentiating* competencies.

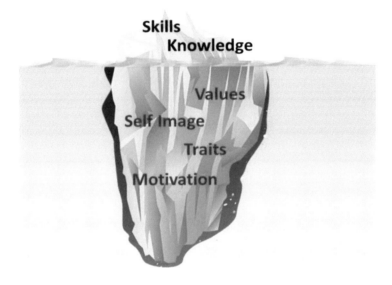

Figure 4.9 – The Iceberg Competency Model (McClelland).

This is relatively straightforward for one role but, inevitably, things become much more complex when organizations attempt to build a system of competency descriptions (a framework) which embraces all employees. In most cases this 'system' takes the form of a matrix which sets the high level competency definitions against the organizational role levels and then defines what that competency means in terms of observable behaviour for each level.

	Level1	Level 2	Level 3	Level 4
Comp A	A	A+1	A + 2	NA
Comp B	B	B + 1	B + 2	B + 3
Comp C	C	C + 1	NA	NA
Comp D	D	D + 1	D + 2	D + 3
Comp E	E	E + 1	E + 2	E + 3

Figure 4.10 – fundamental competency framework concept.

Most frameworks will describe each competency in general terms and then provide a range of behavioural descriptors which enable the observer to distinguish between unsatisfactory, satisfactory and exceptional performance. These descriptors are intended to provide a standardized language to support recruitment, development, performance management, succession planning and remuneration processes.

Building an effective competency framework requires considerable expertise. Consequently many organizations choose to buy in expertise to do this for them, or to take on a generic frameworks designed and maintained by specialist providers such as Lominger or KornFerry.

References.

1. See. Oxford University Press. 2016 at *http://www.oxforddictionaries.com/words/does-english-have-most-words*

2. Carroll, G. Boutall, T. (2011). *A Guide to Developing National Occupational Standards*. Available at *www.comprocom.eu/library. Page 20.*

3. See *http://www.ilo.org/public/english/bureau/stat/isco/isco88/major.htm*

4. See *http://www.jobbank.gc.ca/es_all-eng.do?index=C*

5. See *https://www.onetonline.org/find/*

6. For a general discussion of the 5 Factor Model see
http://www.personalityresearch.org/papers/popkins.html

7. Hay Group Working Paper. Available at:
http://www.haygroup.com/downloads/uk/competencies_and_high_p
erformance.pdf

8. See McClelland, D.C. (1973). *Testing for competence rather than
intelligence.* American Psychologist. *28*, pp. 1–14

5

Capacity issues – how many people? Sustaining business as usual.

Defining capacity.

As noted earlier, 'capacity' can be thought of as *sufficiency* i.e. have we got *enough* of the capable people we need to sustain the business? Superficially this sounds simple enough, but the practice of monitoring capacity involves learning from the past, monitoring the present and projecting into the future. It also requires access to rich HR and operational data in order to perform the necessary analytical exercises.

Capacity, like capability is never likely to be static. For example, technological change, significant product or service variation or budgetary considerations will inevitably impact the numbers of people deemed necessary or supportable. Many of these variables are related to organizational strategy and therefore are future-focused. Others, such as reductions in headcount, driven by cost-cutting imperatives, may be entirely reactive and intended for immediate implementation. For the purposes of this section we shall focus on maintaining the operational status quo. Therefore the assumption is that the present workforce needs to be sustained for the foreseeable future.

Identifying and mitigating risk.

Identifying the degree of capacity risk resident within a workforce is essentially no different to any other risk environment. It is matter of *likelihood* versus *consequence* i.e. what are the chances of this event occurring, and, if it did, how bad would it be? With older employees the likelihood of loss of capacity in a given role is governed by factors such as proximity to retirement age or perhaps deteriorating physical abilities. With younger employees likelihood is negatively affected by factors such as limited internal progression or better prospects elsewhere (flight risk). Factors that would mitigate flight risk would include no viable alternatives and domestic impedances to free movement; such as a spouse well entrenched in his /her own career, children at critical stages in their schooling etc.

Aging workforce.

The biggest single risk facing businesses today is dealing with the aging workforce and the exit of the baby boomers. Those organizations that are failing to deal with this issue strategically are already experiencing severe difficulties in maintaining both capability and capacity. What is needed is a relatively simple method of identifying the 'hot spots' in the workforce landscape i.e. those roles that are highly skilled and are likely to see individuals exiting. We shall look at a simple three-stage process that provides this information at an individual and an organizational level.

Stage 1 - involves getting to grips with the historical landscape. Organizations that are relatively stable i.e. are not affected by significant 'churn' or consistent change in the workplace environment, will offer an historical profile that can be usefully extrapolated into the future to provide a realistic sense of what is coming down the line. We need to understand the drivers and patterns of staff turnover. The key questions to be asked are:

- What is the average age of retirement (countries with mandatory retirement ages will have this information as a certainty).
- On average, how many dismissals occur each year.
- On average, how many resignations do we have each year.
- On average, how many medical retirements are made each year.
- On average, how many deaths in service do we have each year.
- On average how many promotions to other roles are made each year.

This information should be available from HR and business unit records. Going back ten years should provide an adequate picture. We should be able to assume that the informing workforce metrics from the last decade will look (overall) very like those for the next. We should be able to extrapolate forward and build a reasonably accurate set of expectations.

Figure 5.1 below shows a typical extrapolation of data gathered from the decade 2004-2014. The average age of retirement was found to be 67 and it is therefore relatively easy to predict numbers retiring, based on their dates of birth. Of course this will never be an exact science but it is a fair assumption based on what the business has experienced.

Total Workforce = 1582																					
Assumed retirment age 67																					
	2014		2015		2016		2017		2018		2019		2020		2021		2022		2023		Acc % of
	No.	%	No	%	No.	%	No.	%	No.	%	No.	%	No.	%	No.	%	No.	%	No.	%	workforce.
Number reaching retirement age.	21	1.33	30	1.9	47	2.97	48	3.03	58	3.67	33	2.09	43	2.72	32	2.02	35	2.21	49	0	21.93426043
Annual resignation (repeat 2004-20014)	15	0.95	12	0.76	17	1.07	16	1.01	9	0.57	22	1.39	11	0.7	12	0.76	32	2.02	15	0.95	9.288758968
Annual dismissal (repeat 2004-2014)	2	0.13	1	0.06	3	0.19	2	0.13	0	0	1	0.06	4	0.25	2	0.13	1	0.06	0	0	1.011378003
Annual death in service (repeat 2004-2014)	0	0	2	0.13	3	0.19	1	0.06	0	0	0	0	1	0.06	4	0.25	1	0.06	0	0	0.758533502
Annual medical retirement (repeat 2001-2014)	3	0.19	2	0.13	4	0.25	0	0	4	0.25	2	0.13	0	0	8	0.51	5	0.32	4	0.25	2.022756005
																			Total % workforce turnover		35.01568691

Figure 5.1 – Example of data extrapolation to predict probable turn-over levels.

You will note that, in this case, when extrapolating the data for resignations, dismissals etc. the business has chosen to repeat the pattern of the previous decade rather than simply spread an average figure equally across the years. In practice either method works just as well. Once again, we could not expect an exact repeat, but over a ten year period we could certainly have some faith in the degree of staff turnover and where the spikes are most likely to occur. Not an exact science but far better than doing nothing. It is certainly a *naïve* form of projection, but because of the depth and general consistency of the data it is rather more probabilistic than stochastic. The availability of data such as this will inform workforce planning in terms of overall numbers i.e. when the 'spikes' are most likely to occur. This is certainly helpful but it is nevertheless relatively high level information which does not allow us to deal with the burning platforms. We need ongoing, present day analysis of the roles which are imminently at risk. There are factors which remain imponderable e.g. 'poaching' by other organisations, but we can certainly apply tools to identify those who are most likely to be exiting the business.

Roles at risk analysis.

Shown below is a simple spreadsheet tool devised to assess the risk of an individual leaving the workforce. This would be completed by a person who understands the role, the factors involved and (ideally) knows the individual well – most probably the individual's line manager. The factors that need to be assessed and rated are:

- Age of the incumbent i.e. in relation to the average age of retirement.
- Difficulty in finding a suitable replacement. This could be related to particular technical or physical requirements, unpleasantness of the work or the working environment, requirements to work unsociable hours or shifts etc.
- Complexity of training.

- Difficulty in finding a suitable in-house trainer or training pro-- vider. There may be people around with the technical knowledge and experience but without any aptitude or appetite for training delivery.
- Length of induction and required training.
- Time needed to reach full productivity.
- Health status of incumbent. This may of course be entirely invisible. Nevertheless, a line manager should have a reliable understanding of the individual's health record and be able to make reasonable assumptions.
- The likelihood of imminent retirement or resignation. Again this may be 'invisible' in as much as the individual does not wish to divulge personal plans, in which case it is best rated neutrally. Other individuals may be happy to share their retirement plans. In any case it is always worthwhile managers having these conversations with their team members.

Figure 5.2 below shows a simple risk rating tool aimed at individuals in specific roles. A 1-10 scale is used, with 1 being no discernible risk and 10 being extreme. Scores are totaled, converted to a percentage and then related to a risk scale. In this example we can see that this individual scores 44% and is therefore regarded as a 'low moderate' risk and therefore unlikely to be an immediate priority in terms of forward training individuals to ensure sufficient contingency in this operational area.

In this example the most significant issues are around the complexity of training and the availability of suitable trainers. If not dealt with adequately, the risk level will inevitably increase. The regular update of these individualized profiles (at least annually) will allow managers to identify a wide range of related issues and to take appropriate steps to reduce their impact.

Complex and lengthy training is invariably linked to more senior roles and these tend, quite naturally to be more critical to ongoing operations e.g. senior energy plant operators on a major manufacturing site. Operations would quickly founder without consistent energy supply. Conversely, roles that require minimal training and allow the individual to come up to speed quickly represent relatively little risk because they can generally be quickly replaced e.g. fork lift drivers in a load-out section. Incumbents of senior roles who are approaching retirement age or experiencing prolonged ill-health clearly represent significant risks. These are the real 'hot spots' in the workplace planning environment. Urgent action must be taken to dampen them down.

Role - Example

Risk Factors	Risk Rating									
	1	2	3	4	5	6	7	8	9	10
Difficulty in finding suitable replacement.	0	0	0	0	5	0	0	0	0	0
Length of induction and training.	0	0	0	0	0	0	7	0	0	0
Time to come up to full speed.	0	0	0	0	0	0	0	8	0	0
Complexity / difficulty of training.	0	0	0	0	0	0	7	0	0	0
Availability of suitable training / trainers.	0	0	0	0	0	0	0	0	9	0
Current age of incumbent.	0	2	0	0	0	0	0	0	0	0
Health status of incumbent.	0	0	0	4	0	0	0	0	0	0
Likelihood of iminent retirement / resignation of incumbent.	0	2	0	0	0	0	0	0	0	0
Column Totals	0	4	0	4	5	0	14	8	0	0
Final total / 80	35									
% exposure	44									

Interpretation of scores	Score	Risk Rating
	80+	Extreme
	70-79	High
	60-69	
	50-59	Moderate
	40-49	
	30-39	Low
	20-29	
	0-19	Insignificant

Figure 5.2 – Example of an individualized roles at risk analysis.

Gathering this information should be delegated to those with the most intimate knowledge of the role in question and of the individual's circumstances. Most often this would be the line manager. It is important to standardize the process by providing descriptors for each of the risk factors. The table below illustrates guidelines that would accompany the risk rating tool at figure 5.2.

1	Difficulty in finding suitable replacement.	Refer to complexity of role + historical experience of recruiting.
2	Length of induction and training.	<ul><li>1 set of shifts = rating of 1</li><li>4 sets of shifts = rating of 3</li><li>10 sets of shifts = rating of 5</li><li>25 sets of shifts = 7</li><li>45 sets of shifts (1 year) = rating of 10</li></ul>
3	Time to come up to full speed.	Estimated time to optimum performance. Based on historical average.
4.	Complexity / difficulty of training.	Estimation of relative technical content (in comparison to other roles).
5.	Availability of suitable training / trainers.	<ul><li>2 or more trainers available = rating of 0</li><li>1 trainer available = rating of 5</li><li>0 trainers available = rating of 10</li></ul>
6.	Current age of incumbent.	<ul><li>65+ = rating of 10</li><li>60-64 = rating of 8</li><li>55-59 = rating of 6</li><li>45-54 = rating of 4</li><li>35-44 = rating of 2</li><li>Up to 34 = rating of 0</li></ul>
7	Health status of incumbent.	Estimation based on available knowledge and sickness / attendance history.
8	Likelihood of imminent retirement / resignation of incumbent.	Time to proposed retirement (if known). <ul><li>Imminent = rating of 10</li><li>Within 3 years = rating of 8</li><li>Within 5 years = rating of 6</li></ul>

		• Within 10 years = rating of 4
		• More than 10 years = rating of 2

Monitoring and reporting risk at site or organizational level.

Senior management are unlikely to be focused on individual roles. They will need a more comprehensive understanding of the risk to operational continuity. This can be achieved through consolidating the individualized roles at risk analysis into the organizational or site 'heat map'. This level of analysis can provide senior managers with a 'one stop shop' overview of the whole workforce risk situation.

Figure 5.3 overleaf provides a typical example of a site heat map. The analysis considers the following factors:

- *Current establishment*: the number employees that the business believes is required for each role under normal running.

- *Optimum skilled*: the number, including the establishment, that is required to cover for leave, sickness, secondments etc. essentially this is a contingency calculation.

- *Current skilled*: the number actually fully trained and able to perform the role.

- *First rating*: the average of role at risk ratings for all incumbents of a given role. This is referred to as the 'first' rating because the level of actual risk will be increased if the optimum skilled number falls below that required.

- *Risk multiplier*: the degree to which the first rating risk may be increased if the optimum skilled number falls short. This is calculated by dividing the optimum skilled number by the current skilled number.

- *Final rating*: calculated, in the spreadsheet, by multiplying the first rating by the risk multiplier. For example, in figure 5.3 we can see that the Run Time Operator role in the Compound Preparation Section is established for 5 operators. To cover all eventualities it has been decided that a total (including the establishment of 10 trained operators are required. Currently only 6 are trained i.e. only one 'spare' to cover the established run time operators. Averaged individual assessments of the operators has produced a first rating of 67%. The risk multiplier works out at 1.67 and this produces a final rating of 111.67%. This takes this role firmly into the red (extreme) zone and signals to management that they have a serious issue that must be addressed.

- *Average risk rating*: this is a useful headline number that can be used to describe trending risk and the success (or failure) of risk management strategies such as succession planning and training interventions.

Heat maps of this kind are powerful tools with which HR can focus the attention of senior management. They capture the present but also point to clear implications for the future. Most importantly, individual line managers can be teamed with HR to attack localized staffing issues in tactically coherent manner.

The continuing potency of this approach does however depend entirely on planned maintenance of the data stream. In most situations this would be too onerous a task for HR to sustain unaided. In addition, HR are not likely to be close enough to the data source (the operational staff themselves) to make appropriate judgments at the first rating stage. The most sensible solution therefore is to formally delegate the first rating task to line managers, supervisors, training coordinators etc. – anybody who is in regular working contact with the individuals concerned. Ideally first ratings should be updated every 6 months and passed to HR who can then refresh the site / department heat maps.

XYZ Acoustic Pads - Roles at Risk Analysis		Risk Rating					Current Establishment	Optimum Skilled	Current Skilled	First Rating	Risk Multiplier	Final Rating
Work Area	Operator Role	Extreme	High	Moderate	Low	Insignificant						
Power Generation	Senior Contro Room Operator						5	8	5	39	1.6	62.4
	No 2 Control Room Operator						6	9	6	39	1.5	58.5
Compound Prep	Senior Mixer / Tester						5	8	10	31	0.8	24.8
	No. 2 Mixer / Tester						5	10	8	38	1.25	47.5
	Zone Supervisor						5	10	5	47	2	94
	Run Time Operator						5	10	6	67	1.666667	111.6667
	Spare Operator						1	2	1	59	2	118
	Bulk materials Handler						5	8	5	49	1.6	78.4
	Goods Inwards Receiver						5	10	5	51	2	102
	Training Spare						1	2	1	28	2	56
Heating / Front End	Zone Supervisor						4	8	20	39	0.4	15.6
	Hot Delivery Operator						4	8	20	39	0.4	15.6
	First Belt Operator						8	16	20	47	0.8	37.6
	Roller Setter						8	16	16	42	1	42
	Spare Operator						1	2	1	38	2	76
	Sampler / Tester						1	2	1	35	2	70
Hardening	Zone Supervisor						5	10	10	30	1	30
	Run Time Operator						5	10	13	37	0.769231	28.46154
	Water Cooling Operator						5	10	10	46	1	46
	Sampler / Tester						5	10	6	65	1.666667	108.3333
	Spare Operator						1	2	5	61	0.4	24.4
	Training Spare						1	2	1	44	2	88
Finishing / Warehouse	Zone Supervisor						5	7	6	30	1.166667	35
	Knife Setter						5	8	6	30	1.333333	40
	Packing Operator						5	7	10	25	0.7	17.5
	Stacker Driver						5	10	20	29	0.5	14.5
	Spare Operator						2	2	1	39	2	78
	Customer ID Operator						5	7	5	43	1.4	60.2
	Goods Outward / Stock Management						5	7	8	44	0.875	38.5
										Total risk rating		1618.962
										Average risk rating		59.96154

As at: October 2013

Figure 5.3 – Example of a site 'heat map' demonstrating the geography of roles at risk.

Other factors that may increase risk.

Risk may be significantly increased by the degree of choice open to workers. If the site is located in an area with numerous other job opportunities, management will have to work harder on retention strategies. This might mean on-going monitoring of local 'poaching' potential. Conversely, if the site is isolated and more remotely located, moving on is a much more difficult decision for the individual.

We should also be aware of the 'lemming effect'. When people form socially cohesive groups in the workplace e.g. shift workers, they are likely, in addition to working together, to socialize outside work, play sport together, go fishing together etc. Not surprisingly, when a member of that social group moves on or decides to retire, a number of his / her colleagues may follow.

Alternative reporting formats.

Senior management may prefer not to drill down into the specific detail of roles at risk, requiring only a comparative overview of what is happening. Figure 5.4 below shows a method of displaying data according to perceived criticality of roles. This is a kind of 'traffic light' reporting. Anything in the red zone should make us stop and pay attention.

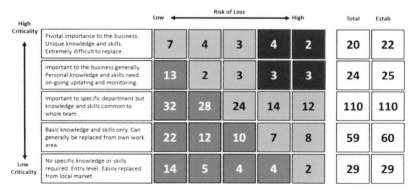

High Criticality		Low	Risk of Loss	High		Total	Estab
	Pivotal importance to the business. Unique knowledge and skills. Extremely difficult to replace.	7	4	3	4	2	20	22
	Important to the business generally. Personal knowledge and skills need on-going updating and monitoring.	13	2	3	3	3	24	25
	Important to specific department but knowledge and skills common to whole team.	32	28	24	14	12	110	110
	Basic knowledge and skills only. Can generally be replaced from own work area.	22	12	10	7	8	59	60
Low Criticality	No specific knowledge or skills required. Entry level. Easily replaced from local market.	14	5	4	4	2	29	29

Figure 5.4 – Traffic light reporting on roles at risk current state.

In this example we can immediately see that the organization is unacceptably exposed to losing a significant tranche of its critical work force. The red zone is showing around 25% of the establishment for important and pivotal roles as being at risk – for whatever reason. Questions must be asked about succession strategies and required contingency. The situation is not much better in parts of the amber zone but those skills can be replaced from within the team. Keeping this analysis current and top of mind for senior management must be viewed as a critical routine for HR departments.

Segmentation or 'localized' monitoring and planning.

Very often, the complexity of data arising from organization or site-wide analysis can effectively obscure the most obvious urgencies and priorities. Line managers will naturally tend to focus on their own immediate areas and may struggle to interpret bigger picture perspectives. If HR is to successfully enlist the help of front line management in gathering information with which to monitor and plan succession and training needs, then more targeted methods will generally have more appeal.

Involving line management in this work is essential, simply because that is where the detailed 'intimate' knowledge of individual circumstances resides. Ideally, the HR professional should adopt the philosophy of 'teaching the man to fish' rather than doing the fishing themselves. This involves encouraging the frontline manager to build monitoring and planning techniques into their critical routines.

Figure 5.5. overleaf shows a simple spreadsheet tool that will enable the manager to track his / her specific workforce in terms of succession needs and key person risk. The various ratings can be regularly and easily updated (perhaps on a quarterly or bi-annual basis) and forwarded to HR for higher level reporting. This is a simple tool that should enable the manager to plan and allocate resources to ensure that the workforce profile is maintained.

Location	Role	Incumbent(s)	Age	Criticality Rating /5	Skills Rating /5	Loss Risk Rating /5	Step up Rating /5	Overall Risk Total	Overall Risk %	Succession / Training Priority
No.2 Pad Plant Morning shift	Warehouse inward operator.	John Harris	56	2	4	1	2	16	2.56	Important 6
	Raw materials storeperson.	Josie Green	52	1	5	2	2	20	3.2	Important 5
	Raw materials line supply operator.	Sefo Tolianu	58	3	3	1	2	18	2.88	
	Raw materials hopper load operator.	Paddy Johns	32	1	2	3	1	6	0.96	
	Batch cook operator.	Hugh Jones	66	4	5	4	5	400	64	Urgent 1
	Tool setter and maintenance operator	Hone Mahanga	68	4	5	5	3	300	48	Urgent 2
	Paper insert feed operator.	Alan McCracken	42	3	3	1	1	9	1.44	
	Stacker operator.	Drew Wilson	38	1	1	1	1	1	0.16	
	Batch ID / customer destination control.	Rav Pradesh	51	4	4	2	3	96	15.36	Important 4
	Fork lift operator (1)	Dion Brown	22	1	2	3	1	6	0.96	
	Fork lift (2)	Micky Taylor	31	1	2	2	1	4	0.64	
	Packing Operator (1)	Vladislaw Czir	56	1	1	1	1	1	0.16	
	Packing Operator (2)	Tui Skerrigs	47	4	4	5	4	320	51.2	
	Warehouse outward operator.	Graham Bolden	69	4	4	5	4	320	51.2	
	Truck loading supervisor.	Wiremu Hastie	48	3	4	2	3	72	11.52	Important 3
No.2 Pad Plant Afternoon shift	Warehouse inward operator.	Geoff Hurst	38	2	3	1	1	6	0.96	
	Raw materials storeperson.	Lisa Moore	43	1	4	2	1	8	1.28	
	Raw materials line supply operator.	Sandy Reynolds	45	3	4	1	1	12	1.92	
	Raw materials hopper load operator.	James Logan	32	1	3	3	1	9	1.44	
	Batch cook operator.	Manu Tualigi	51	4	5	2	4	160	25.6	Important 5
	Tool setter and maintenance operator	Peter Reece	66	4	5	5	5	500	80	Urgent 1
	Paper insert feed operator.	Keith Nelson	48	3	3	2	3	54	8.64	
	Stacker operator.	Eli Wilson	52	1	3	1	1	3	0.48	
	Batch ID / customer destination control.	Angie Jessup	53	4	5	3	4	240	38.4	Important 3
	Fork lift operator (1)	Ken Leitch	57	1	4	1	1	4	0.64	
	Fork lift (2)	Ross Williams	32	1	3	1	1	3	0.48	
	Packing Operator (1)	Rosie Davies	33	1	3	1	1	3	0.48	
	Packing Operator (2)	Hugh Jenkins	46	1	1	1	1	1	0.16	
	Warehouse outward operator.	Neil Thomas	67	4	5	5	4	400	64	Important 2
	Truck loading supervisor.	Aaron Porter	54	3	4	2	3	72	11.52	Important 5

Figure 5.5 – Monitoring / planning tool for succession and prioritization of training.

This example relates to a 2 shift (morning and afternoon) process operation. The following criteria are routinely observed, noted and rated.

- **Incumbent age** – highly significant because the risk of loss (temporary or permanent) increases as people age and approach retirement.
- **Criticality rating** – refers to the relative importance of the role to the operation as a whole. These roles are usually the more technical functions that require greater time for training. Rated on a scale of 1-5 with 5 being highly critical.
- **Skills rating** – refers to the current level of skill demonstrated by the incumbent (see team skills matrix example at figure 4.9). A high rating means that the individual has attained a high level of competence in the role and loss is therefore potentially more significant.
- **Loss risk rating** - estimates the likelihood of the incumbent retiring, being medically downgraded or retired, choosing to leave the role or the organization etc. A high rating signified high likelihood.
- **Step-up rating** – refers to the current availability of individuals trained, able and willing to move into the role. A high rating indicates high risk i.e. limited or zero contingency.
- **Overall risk total** – multiplies the criteria to achieve a total i.e. 5x5x5x5 = 625.
- **Overall risk %** - converts the total to a more comprehensible percentage.
- **Succession / training priority** – the risk % are then colour coded as in terms of their importance and urgency and ranking inserted.

Armed with this information the line manager and HR can approach succession, recruitment and training in an informed manner. This is particularly crucial when resources are constrained.

Identifying critical roles.

Of course all roles are of some importance, but there those that are undoubtedly more critical for on-going success. These are the potential red zone people. So how can we identify these roles? Different organizations will have specific criteria that inform these decisions, but there are key questions that will always occur. The questionnaire below is a useful basis for this exercise.

	Key Criteria	Not at all	Not significantly	Significantly	Critically
	If we lost continuity in this role it would	1	2	3	4
1.	- negatively impact the leadership or supervision of a department or functional area.	☐	☐	☐	☐
2.	- negatively impact the functional area's ability to achieve / maintaining quality or quantity targets.	☐	☐	☐	☐
3.	- negatively impact the upskilling and development of other important staff.	☐	☐	☐	☐
4.	- negatively impact the ability of other staff to perform as required?	☐	☐	☐	☐
5.	- negatively impact the organisation's ability to build / maintain important internal or external relationships.	☐	☐	☐	☐
6.	- negatively impact health and safety in the functional area.	☐	☐	☐	☐
7.	- negatively impact planned major projects.	☐	☐	☐	☐
8.	- negatively impact the organisation's competitive advantage.	☐	☐	☐	☐
9.	- negatively impact the on-going maintenance of systems and processes.	☐	☐	☐	☐
10.	- negatively impact the ability to problem-solve and implement solutions in the functional area.	☐	☐	☐	☐
	Column totals				
	Final total				

Obviously, an individual role is unlikely to return high criticality ratings across all these criteria. Indeed it may be that the loss of continuity in a role appears to be highly significant in only one area. Consequently we should assume that a rating of 4 for any of these key criteria indicates a level of criticality that needs to be investigated and ultimately mitigated. Naturally, overall criticality mounts if the role impacts a number of these criteria. A final total of 20-30 should be regarded as representing a significant risk and a score of 30+ regarded as a 'burning platform'. These roles are truly 'critical' by which we mean that failing to maintain the continuity of the role could result in the organization or business unit failing to achieve its objectives or a significant degrading of operations.

Critical roles can exist at any level within the organization, but of course are more likely to occur where requirements exist for specialized skills or rare experience. In the same way that we must guarantee a 'leadership pipeline' we must build a continuum for the replacement of all our critical roles.

Planning for succession and contingency.

So far, we have described tools and processes for identifying roles at risk and, within that group, roles that should be regarded as critical. We now need to look at how we guarantee status quo overall operational performance (or better) into future. Of one thing we may be certain; if this is not purposefully managed both capacity and capability will eventually be compromised. This is akin to the second law of thermodynamics i.e. (without intervention) "all processes manifest a tendency toward decay and disintegration".

'Intervention' should take the form of ongoing monitoring of performance levels and accompanying assessments of potential to move vertically or horizontally to other roles or new levels within the same role. Clearly, there are a number of permutations in this relationship. The 9 Box Tool shown overleaf at figure 5.5 represents these permutations in matrix form and allows us to think clearly about the relative positioning of team members. Performance and potential are assessed simply as either low, moderate or high. Naturally, these judgments should be supported by sound on-going performance management processes that will generate sufficient detail to enable confident appraisal.

Each permutation is equated with a characterization e.g. 'the rough diamond'. These help to bring the matrix to life. In most cases this is a tool that is used in confidence by a manager or perhaps in consultation with HR business partners who may be assisting with the succession planning process.

		PERFORMANCE	
	LOW	**MODERATE**	**HIGH**
HIGH	Low Performer + High Potential "The rough diamond"	Moderate Performer + High Potential "Future star"	High Performer + High Potential "Leading light"
MODERATE	Low Performer + Moderate Potential "Just on the radar"	Moderate Performer + Moderate Potential "Core employee"	High Performer + Moderate Potential "Current star"
LOW	Low Performer + Low Potential "The wrong'un"	Moderate Performer + Low Potential "Getting there"	High Performer + Low Potential "Steady as she goes"

(POTENTIAL — vertical axis)

Figure 5.6 – The 9 Box Tool for performance monitoring and succession planning

The 9 box analysis invariably begins life as a snapshot of the current situation within a team, but in the hands of a proactive manager it quickly evolves into a tracking tool and a means of identifying development needs. In reality, many managers will not be aware of tools such as this and will need to be coached by HR in its use. Standard guidelines on how to interpret, and subsequently populate the grid should be issued to all managers to ensure a common understanding. A definitions table is offered below.

The "Wrong'un".	**Low performer, low potential.** If this behaviour is consistently observed, it's time to admit that we have the wrong person in the job. Poor recruiting is most likely the issue here. This individual should be performance managed out of the team or redeployed to a more suitable role. Development is likely to meet with little reward and resources are far better expended elsewhere.
"Just on the radar"	**Low performer, moderate potential.** This individual could do better, but for some reason is not. Investigate the cause. If necessary consider doing some coaching toward the modest improvement anticipated. If this fails, performance manage to expected levels. Don't set the bar too high. Try to encourage success via a campaign of 'small victories'.
"Rough diamond"	**Low performer, high potential.** This individual is likely to be very frustrating for managers and for team-mates alike. They have considerable ability but for some reason are not living up to their potential. This is a significant waste of talent and investigation is needed to unearth the issues. Causes can vary from boredom (been in the job too long) to disenchantment, relationship issues, or the failure of the manager to clarify expectations adequately. If stagnation is the cause, performance management should focus on potential career development or role exchange accompanied by relevant development activity.
"Getting there"	**Moderate performer, low potential.** This individual is probably reaching their ceiling in their current role with little apparent ability to develop further. Consider re-deployment or peer coaching. Again, don't set the bar too high.
"Core employee"	**Moderate performer, moderate potential.** This individual is the classic 'middle of the roader'. Probably fairly happy with their lot? Development should be targeted on a limited raising of the game in the same role. Performance targets

	should require some stretch activity but not be unrealistic given limited potential. Re-deployment may be an option if the individual shows interest in progression.
"Future star"	Moderate performer, high potential. This person has more to give and is clearly willing to offer it. Consequently, development should be geared to an exploration of what standard could reasonably be attained and aligned to the individual's personal aspirations. ROI on development is likely to be high.
"Steady as she goes"	High performer, low potential. Be grateful here. You are getting the best out of somebody who has little potential to go further (in this role at least). Significant development activity will most likely be unsuccessful and failure may de-motivate. Clear maintenance objectives are the order of the day, accompanied by positive response to on-going high performance.
"Current star"	High performer, moderate potential. Clearly a highly motivated individual who has room for further development. It is important to recognize the limitations here because failure to meet new standards could seriously discourage and lead to a fall-off in performance.
"Leading light"	High performer, high potential. This individual is the beacon in your team. A role model of how things should be done and of the drive to personally improve. While managers should rejoice in having such people in their teams, they should also be hearing the alarm bells. This person is at their peak in their present role and has the ability to do more – but most likely in a different role? Commonly, these are the people selected to move into supervisory or leadership roles. If neglected, these individuals are undoubtedly flight risks.

The 9 box grid should be viewed as a 'living' document. After initially populating the matrix managers should use it to strategize and plan development activity. Top of mind must be the flow through into roles identified as critical for operational continuity or quality performance.

Figure 5.6 below gives an example of the grid populated for a team of 16. In this case the manager has identified critical roles by the letter C after their names. Colour-coding might be an alternative option. We can see immediately that there are issues to be attended to here. While Malcolm D and Leslie H may be leading lights they are also in critical roles. The manager must be aware of the potential flight risk here. She must also take the opportunity, while they are present in the team, to 'download' their knowledge, and hopefully their attitudes to those who might step up e.g. Kaycie J, Geoff M, Trevor G and Neil A.

Another clear problem here is John R, identified as a rough diamond in a critical role. He is not performing to his potential and needs to be brought up to speed quickly. Meanwhile John D needs to be replaced by somebody more suitable.

		PERFORMANCE		
		LOW	**MODERATE**	**HIGH**
POTENTIAL	**HIGH**	*"The rough diamond"* John R (C)	*"Future star"* Kaycie J Geoff M	*"Leading light"* Malcolm D (C) Leslie H (C)
	MODERATE	*"Just on the radar"*	*"Core employee"* Lynn M, Ron B Will J (C) Brian B , Keith M.	*"Current star"* Trevor G, Neil A
	LOW	*"The wrong'un"* John D	*"Getting there"* Richie B	*"Steady as she goes"* Ben T, Paul S, Sheila N, Lee S, Shane N

Figure 5.7 – example of a populated 9 box grid.

A strategic approach to succession planning.

The forecasting of talent supply needs to be embraced as an integrated approach i.e. jointly combining research into what skills are already available or latent *within* the organization with a determined and ongoing scrutiny of what is available from *external* sources.

We have already looked briefly at succession planning tools in the light of internal progression. It is possible to extend these tools somewhat further to include additional levels of potential. The most usual approach is a version of the Markov analysis which assists the prediction, from year to year, of staff who are likely to remain in their present roles, be promoted or demoted, transfer to other business units or exit. Essentially this is a living process which provides for longer term tracking of internal skills supply. Most organizations are necessarily quite fluid, often exhibiting 'ripple effects' caused by staff movements. The Markov analysis allows HR and line managers to get ahead of the game and to use these dynamics proactively. In a quite obvious way it supports a 'grow your own' philosophy, but also reflects the need to identify and remove 'dead wood'.

The Markov analysis is 'strategic' in the sense that it demands a systematic bringing together of processes aimed at providing a conscious view of the *potential* offered by the internal workforce. In this sense it is future-focused.

The most critical of these processes is undoubtedly performance management. Completion of a Markov is impossible without reference to data emerging from the in-house performance management system. This data enables decisions to be made regarding promotability or, conversely demotion and perhaps the need to exit people from the business.

Figure 5.8 below shows a typical Markov analysis for a fictional manufacturing firm.

To \ From (Validated number)	Plant Manager (1)	Area Manager (3)	Plant Engineer (3)	Technical Manager (4)	Technical Supervisor (12)	Shift Supervisor (5)	Charge Hand (15)	Senior Machine Operator (32)	Junior Machine Operator (160)	General Hand (82)	Projected Supply Risk (succession)	Column Ref
Business Unit Manager	0% (0)	33% (1)									L	A1, A2
Area Manager	0% (0)	66% (2)	66% (2)								L	B1, B2
Plant Engineer		0% (0)	33% (1)	0% (0)							H	C1, C2
Technical Manager			0% (0)	75% (3)	17% (2)						L	D1, D2
Technical Supervisor				0% (0)	66% (8)	20% (1)					M	E1, E2
Shift Supervisor					8% (1)	60% (3)	6% (1)				H	F1, F2
Charge Hand						20% (1)	80% (12)	16% (5)			M	G1, G2
Senior Machine Operator							0% (0)	78% (25)	5% (8)		L	H1, H2
Junior Machine Operator								3% (1)	83% (133)	13% (11)	L	J1, J2
General Hand									10% (16)	78% (64) N/A		K1, K2
Exits	0% (0)	0% (0)	0% (0)	25% (1)	8% (1)	0% (0)	13% (2)	3% (1)	2% (3)	8.00% (7)		L1, L2

Figure 5.8 – typical Markov analysis

Certain conditions are essential for the application of the Markov approach. Chief among these are:

- An agreed promotion line. This would be the normal progression 'up the ranks'. This is not to deny extraordinary promotions but rather a reflection of the predictable.

- Management willingness to engage with HR on a regular basis to 'refresh' the entries.

The analysis considers and records the answers to four fundamental questions for each role:

1. What proportion (%) of the validated number of incumbents is considered promotable to the next level i.e. in the promotion line)?

2. What proportion is not yet promotable but are competent and likely to remain in their current role?

3. What proportion is regarded as inadequate in their current role and should be *demoted* to a lower level?

4. What proportion is should be performance managed out of the business (exited)?

Pulling this information together allows us to grasp the succession potential and, of course, the roles that are exposed to succession risk.

So, for example, looking at figure 5.8 and the horizontal role row of Technical Manager in particular, we can see the following entries:

- Columns C1 and C2 – set against the vertical role column of Plant Engineer. The validated number of Technical managers is 4 but none (0) is considered worthy or capable of promotion to Plant Engineer.

- Columns D1 and D2 – set against the vertical role column of Technical Manager. 75% i.e. 3 out of the 4 are considered competent in their present role and likely to continue.

- Columns E1 and E2 – set against the vertical role column of Technical Supervisor. The entries indicate that no Technical Managers need to be demoted to Technical Supervisor.

- Columns L1 and L2 (exit consideration) – we can see that the fourth Technical Manager has a poor performance record and is likely to be exited from the business.

Consequently, given that there is no visible 'normal' succession into the Plant Engineer role this is regarded as a High Risk and will require management strategies designed to bring others forward, most likely through the creation of developmental activity.

It is clear that maintaining such an analysis as part of normal business planning (a critical routine) will enable HR business partners to engage with their managers with conviction. The process also allows management to identify issues such as flight risks i.e. when there are insufficient openings for those considered worthy of promotion and to consider options for ensuring retention. Areas of high turnover will also be identified and appropriate questions asked.

Planning developmental activity.

Having identified roles at risk and any critical roles among them, we need now to be thinking in terms of who would be suitable to develop as potential replacements should those roles become vacant. Our heat maps should be able to provide the required contingency factor and allow us to prioritize according to the final risk rating.

Ideally, identifying the most suitable step-up or step across candidates should be a well-considered process rather than a knee-jerk reaction to a crisis. Information such as the required duration of training or developmental activity for the given role should allow managers to plan backwards to effective start points. That start point should include time for an assessment of the individual against the competencies for the new role. For example, if we are considering developing a senior production operator to step into a front line supervisor's role, we should consider his / her present abilities in the light of the supervisor's role map. This will provide an effective gap analysis and assist with the planning of a focused development plan.

Development options.

Formulating the individual's development plan is best done in consultation with a learning and development specialist if possible. If the organization does not possess this expertise, HR should be consulted at the very least. The most important consideration here is that development should be relevant and delivered at the right level.

It is also important that managers do not look for the easy way out and immediately reach for the course catalogue. There are always numerous options to be considered. Front of mind should be the 70:20:10 concept (see figure 5.9 below).

This model formalizes what most L&D professionals have always instinctively understood i.e. there are very often more effective solutions for individual development than formal training or learning programmes. McCall, Lombardo and Eichinger of the Centre for Creative leadership (CCL) developed the idea when researching how people actually learned in the workplace. They found that:

Development generally begins with a realization of current or future needs and the motivation to do something about it. This might come from feedback, a mistake, watching other people's reactions. Failing or not being up to a task – in other words from experience. The odds are that development will be about 70% from on the job experiences – working on tasks and problems; about 20% from feedback and working around good and bad examples of the need; and about 10% from courses and reading. (1)

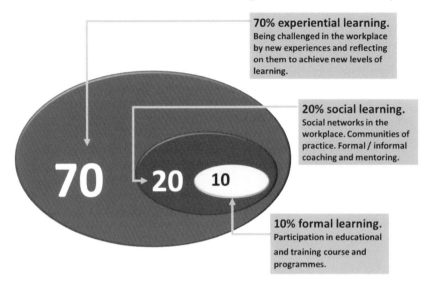

70% experiential learning.
Being challenged in the workplace by new experiences and reflecting on them to achieve new levels of learning.

20% social learning.
Social networks in the workplace. Communities of practice. Formal / informal coaching and mentoring.

10% formal learning.
Participation in educational and training course and programmes.

Figure 5.9 – The 70:20:10 concept.

The model has attracted some criticism on the grounds that it can never be proved to be specifically accurate on terms of those ratios. This is to miss the point entirely. The model is not intended to be pre-scriptive, rather a reasonable guideline to what actually occurs and, in most situations, to what should occur. Few would doubt that learning gained in the real world of the workplace offers greater relevance and value because it is *situated learning* (2) and in many cases will be ap-plied to real issues. The real significance of the 70:20:10 approach is that it encourages managers to think in terms of real world learning as the most natural answer to development needs.

Formal learning, out of the workplace, will always be of value provid-ing it is effective. Ideally, effectiveness needs to be proven before or-ganizations incur the often considerable associated costs. The real issue with learning of this kind is whether it can be transferred to the workplace sufficiently to add value. This is Kirkpatrick's level 3 evalua-tion (3). Fresh perspectives from external sources can encourage organizations to adopt a more objective and less insular self-view, but only if they are sufficiently open and receptive.

A little creative imagination will expose a wealth of potential internal development opportunities. These might include:

- Targeted project work – designed to require the specific skill sets that the individual needs for progression.
- Role shadowing – being assigned to work alongside an acknowledged expert.
- Role exchange / rotation – moving around a team on a planned basis. This is intended to develop individual and team capability and flexibility. This might be possible on an inter-departmental basis or, in the case of major businesses, might take the form of international exchange.
- Role enlargement – the horizontal expansion of the job to include more tasks at the same level of proficiency. This is intended to develop the individual's capacity.
- Role enrichment – a vertical extension of the job to include tasks requiring higher level skills. This is intended to develop the individual's capability.
- 'Research' assignments e.g. process mapping for continuous improvement.
- Leadership opportunities – related to specific team objectives.
- Subject matter expert (SME) attachments to project teams – helps the individual to sharpen their understanding of what they actually know and can do. This can be useful for identifying further technical development needs.
- Coaching – either being coached by more expert colleagues or acting as a coach themselves.
- Mentoring – working with the more experienced colleague / individual to develop a more balanced view of the workplace, its constraints and its opportunities.

References:

1. Lombardo, M. Eichinger, R. 1996. *The Career Architect Develop- ment Planner.* Page   4. Lominger.
2. See: Lave, J. Wenger, E. 1990. *Situated Learning: Legitimate Pe- ripheral participation.* Cambridge University Press.
3. See: Kirkpatrick, D. Kirkpatrick J. 1994. *Evaluating Training Pro- grams.* Berrett-Koehler Publishers.

6

Increasing sophistication – exploiting metrics and scenario modeling.

As we have seen, historical HR data can be extrapolated into the future to provide an indication of *what* is likely to happen within the workforce. This is the traditional or 'basic' approach to workforce planning. However, we should admit that this is a somewhat two dimensional view of the world. HR departments will be better placed to advise their senior managers if they have some understanding of *why* these events are likely to occur. Achieving this level of understanding is largely a matter of acute observation and analysis of key HR metrics relevant to workforce planning, that are generally easily obtained, providing the organization maintains a competent HRIS.

A basic HR metrics framework.

Firstly, as an HR professional, it is important to have a clear view of the HR metrics framework and then to be able to select those measures that will increase the transparency of workforce sustainability issues. The table below provides an overview of the HR metrics framework.

Metrics Group	Tool ID	Purpose
1.Productivity	1.1 -Revenue per	To identify the relationship between revenue and the number of FTE em-

Productivity cont.	FTE	ployees. Useful in identifying potential recruitment 'bloat'.
	1.2 - Profit per FTE	To identify final profit generated per FTE employee. Useful in monitoring improving or failing workforce efficiency trends.
	1.3 - Human capital ROI	To identify the profit generated for each dollar of FTE employee compensation. Useful in assessing the effectiveness of HR, deployment and development practices.
	1.4 - Absenteeism rates	To identify the average number of work days / shifts across the workforce. Useful in identifying potential significant health, performance management or engagement issues.
2. Compensation	2.1 - Labour cost per FTE	To identify and monitor the relationship between all costs associated with employing FTEs and total business expenditure. Useful for early identification of labour cost 'creep'.
	2.2 - Labour cost to revenue %	To identify total labour costs as a % factor of total revenue. Useful as an ongoing indicator of the effectiveness of pay for performance systems.
	2.3 - Labour cost expense %	To identify the proportion of overall expenses that are consumed by labour costs. Useful for monitoring potential impact of changing labour costs on profitability.
3. Recruitment	3.1 - Vacancy rate	To identify the % of roles undergoing active recruitment at the end of each reporting period. Useful for providing early warnings of labour supply issues.
	3.2 -Time to fill	To identify trends in labour supply 'lag'. Used in conjunction with vacancy rates and any need to re-focus or re-energize recruitment strategies.
	3.3-First year res-	To identify the % of employees who

	ignation rates.	move on after less than one year in post. Useful for highlighting quality of recruitment or on-boarding issues. May also be a retention issue or perhaps serious issues of leadership, or team morale.
4. Retention	4.1 - Turnover	To identify the % of employees exiting the organization within the reporting period. Needs to be broken down into rates for resignations, retirements, dismissals etc. Also needs to be considered in the light of what is 'normal' for the type of organization and locality.
	4.2 - Voluntary turn-over	A specific metric within the turnover rate. Identifies those who choose to leave. Useful for identifying potential issues relating to engagement, management practices, lack of development opportunity, salary competitiveness etc.
	4.3 - Overall resignation rate	To quantify the number of people choosing to leave as % of total headcount. Useful as an indicator of the effectiveness of retention strategies, compensation etc. but must be related to context e.g. within an ageing workforce rates may increase significantly due to health issues etc.
	4.4-Resignation rate by age group	To identify issues that may be related to workforce generations. Useful for indicating whether more needs to be done to engage, motivate and retain a specific age group.
	4.5 – Exit intelligence.	To identify any trends in the motivation for resignations – particularly of critical roles.
	4.6-Resignation rate re roles designated as 'critical'.	To identify and monitor the rate at which the business is losing critical talent.

	4.7-Locations of resignation categories.	To monitor the 'spread' of resignation activity across the business. Will identify problem areas for investigation.
	4.8 - Overall retirement rate.	To identify the % of the total workforce that opt to take retirement at or after the age of qualification. Organizations may wish to retard this (to retain expertise) or to accelerate it (to reduce the average age).
	4.9 - Average retirement age	To forecast likely 'spikes' in turnover and to facilitate associated succession planning.
5. Succession	5.1 – succession planning performance	To identify and monitor the % of critical roles supported by active succession planning.
6. Workforce demographics	6.1 - Average age	To identify and monitor the average age across the workforce. Useful for informing the required balance between required experience and expertise and the need to contain costs associated with an older workforce. Should be differentiated by work type, department activity etc.
	6.2 - Gender / diversity mix	To identify actual diversity levels relative to stated organizational policy / needs.
	6.3 - Union membership	To monitor trends in membership. Periods of significant increase may indicate dis- satisfaction and low levels of engagement.

It is easy to see that a wide range of questions could be answered if all this information was to hand. Unfortunately, few organizations are sufficiently well resourced to generate comprehensive data on a consistent basis – and then make sense of it.

Once we have a clear view of the range of metrics available we need to select those that will be of direct use to us in terms of workforce planning. As we have seen, there are levels of relative 'maturity' associated with workforce planning. Most sizeable organizations will, of necessity, engage in the most basic 'traditional' processes of planned headcount replacement, but this alone can be surprisingly erratic without additional levels of data interrogation. Many HR professionals, when asked why they have not moved to higher levels, will simply admit that they don't know how, and not knowing how is due to the fact that there seems to be no process they can follow - plenty of bewildering statistical methods but no stepping stone path to follow.

Fig 6.1 overleaf offers just such a pathway, albeit a circular one. The central purpose of the exercise is to arrive at a *workforce strategy*. This is achieved firstly by using our HR data to answer key questions, beginning with an historical analysis which, if sufficiently extended, can offer rich insights into potential future workforce behaviour. The object of the analytical phase is to produce for senior management a clear view of the present and most likely future trends within the workforce. At this stage the analysis is fundamentally concerned with an assumed status quo, with business as usual.

The second half of the cycle concerns itself with what degree of change should be factored into that primary analysis. The questions here are initially concerned with environmental scanning and scenario modeling in order to reshape the workforce profile and to manage risk effectively.

Criticality of engagement with senior management.

Defining future talent requirements and building a strategy for securing them has now become a defining issue for all organizations, both private and public sector. HR must become a forceful voice at senior management and Board levels. DDI international would go further in maintaining that *"Talent management professionals need to move from a seat at the table to setting the table."* This implies, absolutely, that HR must be integrated fully into the strategic planning process to ensure that the right questions are asked at the appropriate time. In most businesses however, we still find HR planning occurring as a subsequent rather than a simultaneous and complementary processes.

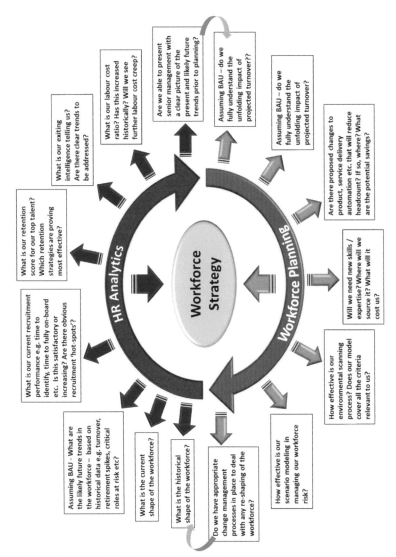

Figure 6.1 – Typical analytics and planning cycle to produce a workforce strategy.

Scenario modeling.

As already noted, our increasingly VUCA world is rapidly rendering any attempt at precise statistical forecasting of staffing requirements more or less futile – some might say obsolete. Who, in 2016, could have foreseen Britain's exit from Europe (BREXIT) or the election of Donald Trump to the American Presidency? Despite their much-lauded statistical and investigative expertise, pretty well all of the polling organizations, and the media got these wrong. Global stock markets priced in the eventualities predicted by the polls and then found themselves having to face an entirely unconsidered reality. Consequently, the focus here is on what is easily achievable by the average HR business partner (working with senior managers), and on what is actually useful i.e. an 'early warning system' regarding all the most likely realities. As we know, forecasting will never be an exact science, but abandoning the attempt is surely irresponsible?

The need for segmentation.

A cautionary note should be voiced here. Most sizeable businesses will be too complex to enable whole of organization scenario modeling. Best practice dictates that we drill down to specific departments or business units that have a clearly distinguishable operational or production focus. At this level we can hope to achieve a degree of precision. This is known as segmentation.

Scenario 1 – BAU steady state ratios.

Reading the runes of an uncertain future must follow the basic rules of navigation i.e. in order to plot a course to a given destination you first need to know (with some certainty) where you are starting from. Invariably the start position is business as usual continuity. The first step, within the specific business unit or department is to review and validate the number of personnel required for each role in normal operational circumstances and the required minimal contingency i.e.

the number required to cover for leave, sickness, special projects etc. Most organizations would optimize their contingency by ensuring that the individuals concerned are multi-skilled and capable of covering a number of bases as required.

A typical steady state analysis might look like the table below. This example is for a paper manufacturing plant.

Business Unit	Role / Function	Validated Number	Minimum Contingency
Paper Plant 1	Business Unit Manager	1	1 (Plant Engineer step up)`
	Area Manager.	3	1 (developmental
	Shift Manager.	5	1 (developmental)
	Stock Preparation Operator	3	1
	Wet End Operator	4	2
	Level 3 Spare Man (Training)	2	0
	Level 3 Spare Man (General Use)	2	1
	Winder Operator	8	2
	Tester / Dryer Assistant	5	2
	Level 2 Spare Man (General Use)	4	2
	Millhand	12	4
	Level 1 Spare Man (General Use)	3	1
	Load Platform Assistant	4	1
	Loud –out Charge Hand	8	2
	Fork Lift Stacker Driver	8	1
	Shunter Driver	3	1
	Warehouse Supervisor	2	0
	Warehouse Operator	4	1

'Validated' number refers to the critical analysis of numbers required historically, tested against optimum operating and safety standards.

'Contingency' is referenced to required leave patterns, historical data regarding average sickness / injury etc. Data should be collected and analyzed regarding the use of contingency staff in order to justify their retention in the workforce.

Properly validated, this steady state data represents the base line requirement going forward. If the business could be certain that nothing would change there would be no deviation from that base line – but a zero change scenario is surely unlikely. The task now is to bring into focus the most likely scenarios for deviation. By and large these are fairly predictable. Figure 6.2 below shows the scenarios that most typically arise. Some would bring about reductions in staffing numbers, others might require temporary or permanent increases.

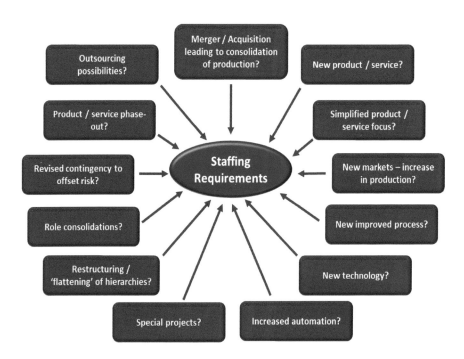

Figure 6.2 – Typical scenarios affecting future staffing numbers.

Mergers and acquisitions.

Changes to workforce capacity and capability during a merger or an acquisition will depend largely on the rationale for the businesses coming together and the nature of their products or services. Businesses are often acquired without an actual merger because their products or services are complementary i.e. they extend or round out the acquirer's portfolio. Acquisitions are often 'trojan horse' strategies for infiltrating new markets via an established reputation. In these cases there may well be no significant impact to the workforces involved, especially if they have been effectively designed and managed. Nevertheless, even in these circumstances, questions will inevitably be asked about synergies and the potential for centralizing and sharing services e.g. IT, HR etc.

Mergers tend to address workforce planning more aggressively. The supporting rationale is most often linked to eradicating competition, moving into new markets or taking advantage of apparent opportunities to 'rationalize' production, support services and, almost always, management and workforces.

Scenario modelling for these events must focus firstly on defining, as precisely as possible, the operational blueprint following the rationalization process. Once we have a clear view of what the new operating model looks like, HR can work with operational managers to identify new or changed capability and capacity requirements. On-going environmental scanning should enable the senior management team to track the various scenarios for possible merger or acquisition, and as a specific scenario begins to emerge as a distinct likelihood, HR can engage with recruiting to identify potential sources of talent. In a world increasingly be-devilled by skills shortages, being ahead of the game will prove critical for operational sustainability.

Restructuring.

Taking a fresh look at how operations actually function and identifying opportunities for more effective use of the workforce, is an exercise that should be conducted on a regular basis as a critical routine for OD/HR and operational managers. The status quo should be constantly challenged. "Restructuring" is perhaps primarily the concern of the OD specialist. Larger organizations may have their own OD staff, but in the majority of cases this work tends to be allocated to consultants but the restructuring exercise is generally reactive rather than an attempt to project to possible future scenarios. Reactive mode implies that the organization can never entirely be the master of its own fate.

Proactive mode can be achieved through the regular review of existing structures and the use of HR analytics (e.g. labour cost to revenue %) to provide base line bench marks. Alternative workforce structures and manning scenarios can then be modelled and perhaps piloted in selected business units or departments and ensuing performance compared to the bench mark analytics. Conducting this kind of work on an on-going basis does, of course, involve the commitment of some resource. Unfortunately, many businesses run so lean that dedicating staff to this kind of analysis is apparently out of the question. The most successful organizations have learned that this success ultimately depends on constant re-creation.

The typical variables to be considered for each structure scenario would be:

- Ratio of management / supervision to individual workers (span of control).
- Required roles in each team.
- Most effective size of teams.
- Possible levels of multi-skilling (reducing the contingency requirement).

- Required support for the business unit e.g. numbers of maintenance staff, IT staff, H&S, HR etc. There are best practice guidelines for these ratios.
- Total labour costs per team. This may increase if higher skill levels are needed, or decrease if contingency factors or required skills levels can be reduced.

New products / services.

While there are those industries whose product lines or services do not change at all, or very slowly, e.g. concrete suppliers, dairy farms, very few could say that there is absolutely no need to think ahead about new products or service offerings. For most businesses, their very survival depends on being in tune with where the market will be - not where it is. The true market leaders will go one step further. They will seek to dictate what the market wants or needs. As Peter Drucker tells us, *"the best way to predict the future is to create it"*.

Clearly there is a very tangible relationship between what is made and the number of people required to make it. Changing product lines will inevitably require analysis of the manufacturing process to determine what labour input is required, based on an assumption that all associated personnel are trained and are up to optimal speed. Once again there are specialists (market analysts) who can advise businesses on what their customers will be wanting in 2, 3, 5 years' time. Given the complexity of contemporary society, their task is undoubtedly becoming more difficult and their findings less reliable. Nevertheless, a few guiding lights in the fog are better than none.

If the product in question has not yet been manufactured (at least to prototype stage) associated labour quantum will be difficult to gauge. Modelling this scenario will require research related to the production of similar items. If the scenario involves potential conversion of plant to extend production of a current line, the calculations should be straightforward, unless new technology is likely to be introduced.

Potential changes in service delivery models will need to be carefully considered if quality (and customer loyalty) is to be maintained. Most scenarios will be driven by the need for greater efficiency or by a potential expansion of service. For example a medical centre might consider reducing the number of home visits made by its doctors in order to use the travelling time involved more effectively by extending the opening hours of the centre and consequently being available to more patients. Similarly, population shifts might provoke a retail business to shift location or open a new branch. The quality of these discussions will of course be dependent on the breadth and depth of environmental scanning undertaken.

Simplified product or service.

Healthy organisations will constantly seek to improve and become more efficient; to do more with less. Continuous improvement asks the question *"is there anything we can stop doing, or providing, that will not damage our relationship with our customers or affect our reputation?"* For example, we are seeing car manufacturers deciding not to install CD players because their customers are increasingly using their personal bluetooth devices to play music through the vehicle sound system. This means that they can reconsider the number of people they employ on that part of the assembly line.

Similarly, companies will regularly review how their sales teams operate. If they are able to reduce the number of face to face visits made by their sales reps, without alienating their customers, they could feasibly operate with a smaller sales team.

New markets or increased production.

Superficially at least, an increase in production or entry into new markets signals an increase in headcount based on current ratios if there is no forseeable changes in plant or process. However, this is not necessarily the case. Questions must be asked about the likely sustainability of the increased demand. Taking on new permanent staff is an expensive process. If there are doubts about sustainability it would probably be more sensible to try to meet demand through overtime working or casual contracts until on-going demand is proven. This solution enables rapid and painless downsizing if required and avoids the additional overheads associated with permanent employees.

Improved processes, technology or automation.

Although these three criteria exhibit different characteristics they all relate to improvements in the way work is done, usually offering an opportunity to reduce specific components of the workforce. Scenarios involving process improvements can be trialled on a small scale and any implications for associated systems fully investigated before moving to formal implementation and shedding of staff. New technology and automation pose rather different problems in that they are not on hand to trial. Scenario modelling here must investigate similar implementations elsewhere, together with the manufacturer's own data to justify pursuing these options to completion.

Role consolidation.

Headcount can be reduced through re-deploying aspects of an individual's role to other individuals who apparently have spare capacity. This often proves to be contentious because it implies that the recipient wasn't fully employed in the first place. Consolidation often becomes a possibility when increased automation or process improvements lighten an individual's workload and enable him / her to take on part of another role which might then be disestablished.

Revised contingency.

In any organization the current workforce will be based on what is seen to be an acceptable level of risk to operational continuity. Management and HR will have arrived at the numbers required to maintain sufficient contingency – but this should never be regarded as a status quo equation. As the workforce ages, we will see people getting sick more often and for longer periods, and perhaps being injured more easily. The most critical roles are often the most difficult to cover. Consequently, HR needs to engage with managers to work through the obvious scenarios around contingency e.g.

- If this critical individual resigns, dies, is long-term sick, or simply goes on leave, do we have somebody able to step up immediately?
- If the covering individual is sick, or on leave when the incumbent is unavailable, how will we cover the role?

Many organizations fail to carry sufficient contingency because they regard it as unnecessary 'fat' in the workforce. That is until they find things grinding to a halt because they cannot back up a critical role. Contingency does not have to equate to supernumerary headcount. It can be designed' into the workforce through strategies such as cross-skilling and role rotation.

Outsourcing.

Permanent employees are expensive to recruit, retain and develop. They drive up a number of non-productive overheads such as pension schemes, health insurance, holiday costs etc. Consequently the option of buying in the labour you need only for as long as you need it and avoiding all of those overheads, is a very attractive one for employers. Of course outsourcing may introduce an element of dependency and uncertainty and these risks need to be assessed during the working of any outsourcing scenario.

Various methods.

If one thing is certain it is that there is no single over-arching formula that will meet the needs of every potential scenario in every organizational context. One size will not fit all. What is needed is the straightforward application of logic to the facts at hand. This is not likely to involve complex statistics. The following scenario examples demonstrate different, but essentially simple approaches to identifying the numbers of employees required to maintain a desired process.

Scenario 2: Modelling required capacity – new technology.

A paper manufacturing company is considering the installation of a new paper machine at one of its sites. The machine incorporates new technology which is significantly different to that which drives the existing machines on site. Management realizes that the staffing ratios from the existing machines should not simply be migrated to the new machine. New calculations are needed to identify the number of process operators needed. Prior to purchasing the new machine a management team visited several other sites where the same plant had been installed and running for some time. Consequently, from detailed observation, it is clear that the machine needs 15 operators, across the various process roles, to run efficiently. All process operator roles are set at the same level, although some individuals may enjoy additional long service payments.

The new machine will be run 24/7 except for 2 planned maintenance shut downs of 1 week each. Operations will be based on a 12 hour shift system, 2 day shifts followed by 2 night shifts, followed by 4 days off. This requires 4 shifts, A,B,C and D working in linked rotation. Operators are expected to take leave during shut down periods when the plant will be handed over to maintenance contractors. The process for calculating the number or operators required to cover all events is as follows:

Step 1: determine the gross workload:

Gross workload = the number of operators required per 24 hour period x the number of days the machine is expected to be running expressed as hours i.e.

15 x 24 x 351 = 128520 man hours per year

Step 2: Determine the available hours (by contract) per operator:

Each operator is expected to work half (12 hours) of each 24 hour period during each 4 day set of shifts. This equates to 25% of each 8 day cycle. Contracted hours therefore equals:

Number of shifts per year (351 / 8 = 43.875) x 48hours = 2106 hours

Step 3: Subtract annual leave entitlement (will be dependent on local agreement). For example:

4 weeks leave (with one week deemed to be 4 rostered shifts off) = 4 x 12hours x 4 = 192 hours

Therefore available hours per operator after annual leave = 2106 – 192 = 1914

Step 4: Subtract statutory holidays entitlement (with each day deemed to be a rostered shifts off).

11 statutory leave days = 11 x 12 =132 hours.

Therefore available hours per operator after stat days = 1914 – 132 = 1782

Step 5: Subtract historical average of sick leave taken + 10 % contingency e.g. 6 rostered shifts

1782 – (6 x12) = 1710 hours individual operator availability.

Step 6: Subtract any standard hours allowed for training e.g. 4 rostered days:

1710 – 48 = 1662 hours individual operator availability

Step 7: Divide gross workload by individual operator availability to identify number of operators required:

128520 / 1662 = 77.6 operators

Conclusion: we can see from this calculation that the superficial requirement of 15 operators for each of the 4 shifts (totaling 60) must be supplemented by an additional 17.6 operators to cover leave and sickness. These numbers can come as a shock to managers, but failing to meet the requirement can lead to serious issues such as staff not being able to take leave, resulting in significant debts building up on the balance sheet; the inability to deliver required training and, potentially, health issues for staff who are unable to take leave. Management may decide to cover some of this additional requirement through overtime or by call-back systems. However, these strategies are never entirely reliable so establishing the roles permanently in order to mitigate risk predictably is often the preferred choice. In that case the issue is how to use the additional personnel profitably when there are few operators on leave or sick. Furthermore, managers would need to ensure that they have sufficient cross-skilling to cover the most critical roles.

Armed with this information management can move to conducting a feasibility study and determine how they would staff the new machine e.g. by migrating experienced operators across from the existing machines on the basis that they will come up to speed quickly, and then back-filling by 'shuffle up' and lower level recruiting from the local labour market.

Scenario 3: Modelling required capacity – contingency % for a steady state business strategy.

Acoustikit Products is a manufacturer of sound-deadening pads used in the automotive industry. Management suspects that the company is carrying too much contingency on its production lines and has instructed HR to 'lean down' manning as far as possible. A segmented approach is to be adopted with each production line being treated as a discrete entity.

The primary production plant which produces the bitumen-based sound insulating sheet material runs on a 48 week year with 2 x 2 week shut downs. To achieve maximum staffing efficiencies and to reduce any residual leave liabilities for the bottom line, all operators are required to take their annual leave during these shut down periods. Production is based on a 2 shift system: morning shift from 6.00 a.m. and an afternoon shift from 2.00 p.m. to 10.00 p.m. Monday to Friday with no planned weekend working.

The process began with primary line number 1. A validation analysis has been conducted to ensure that the minimum numbers are required to run the line under normal operating conditions. HR must provide a calculation that identifies the 'leanest' solution to ensure continuity of production.

Of course "lean" solutions always tread very close to the edge of disaster. Events such as an outbreak of influenza are the extreme end of the planning spectrum because they cannot be foreseen. Most organizations therefore choose to deal to those kinds of risk proactively through strategies such as whole workforce vaccination. What can be foreseen and hopefully managed, are factors such as holiday entitlements, average days off sick etc. When factored into the equation these criteria allow staffing shortfall to be calculated and strategies developed for providing contingency. The spreadsheet below illustrates a practical approach to this problem.

Roles Per Shift (Primary Line 1)	Grade	Validated Minimum	Gross Workload (Annualised Hours)	Stat Hols (Annualised Hours)	Sick Leave Hours	Trg Hours	Available hours	Differential (hours)	Differential (Neg %)
Warehouse Inward Operator	2	4	15360	576	320	96	14371	988.95	93.562
Raw Materials Storeperson	1	2	7680	288	160	48	7138.2	541.76	92.946
Raw Materials Line Supply Operator	2	6	23040	864	480	96	21602	1437.6	93.761
Raw Materials Hopper Load Operator	2	4	15360	576	320	96	14370	989.56	93.558
Batch Cook Operator	3	4	15360	576	320	144	14371	988.95	93.562
Tool Setter and Maintenance Operator	3	2	7680	288	160	144	7138.4	541.56	92.948
Paper Insert Feed Operator	2	4	15360	576	320	96	14370	989.86	93.556
Packer / Stacker Operator	1	8	30720	1152	640	48	28834	1885.6	93.862
Batch ID / Customer Destination Control	2	4	15360	576	320	96	14370	989.76	93.556
Fork Lift Operator	1	6	23040	864	480	48	21602	1437.6	93.761
Warehouse Outward Operator	2	4	15360	576	320	96	14371	988.96	93.561
Truck Loading Supervisor	2	2	7680	288	160	96	7139.1	540.94	92.957
Process Line Manager	6	2	7680	288	160	256	7137.8	542.17	92.941
Process Line Engineer	4	2	7680	288	160	128	7232	448	94.167

Base Info	Shift pattern = 2 x 8 hour shifts Mon - Fri
	Morning shift 6 a.m. - 2 p.m.
	Afternoon shift 2 p.m. - 10 p.m.
	Working year = 48 x 5 day weeks (2 x 2 week shuts) = 240x16 hour days
	Statutory holidays = 9 days

- *Roles per shift* lists the validated functions required to operate the line successfully.
- *Grade* indicates the relative salary levels.
- *Validated minimum* identifies the proven number of staff required to perform each role.
- *Gross workload* calculates (in annualized hours) the availability required over the year i.e.
  Validated minimum x 2 shifts x 8 hours x 240 working days
- *Statutory hols entitlement* calculates the hours not available, in this case 9 working days i.e.

Validated minimum x 2 shifts x 8 hours x 9 working days
- *Sick leave hours* calculates the hours not available due to sickness, in this case based on historical experience of an average of 5 days per role i.e.
Validated minimum x 2 shifts x 8 hours x 5 working days
- *Training hours* calculates the hours not available due to planned release for required training i.e.
Validated minimum x 2 shifts x 8 hours x # of days (variable according to role)
- *Available hours* calculates the number of hours each staff member is available for work after the known deductions i.e. *Gross workload minus stat hols, sick leave hours and training hours*
- *Differential* calculate the shortfall of hours for each role i.e. *Gross workload minus available hours*
- *Differential (neg %)* expresses the shortfall as a negative percentage i.e.
Available hours divided by gross workload x 100

Conclusions:

It is evident from the relatively small negative % differentials that the operation is already running pretty lean. This is undoubtedly due to not having to cover annual leave entitlements (covered off by site-wide annual maintenance shuts). Nevertheless there is an evident risk to be managed here. Employing an additional person to cover each role is surely not an option – most of the time the operation would have people standing around doing nothing. Consequently HR does an additional calculation i.e. summing the negative % differentials for all the operator roles and discovers this amounts to nearly 80%. HR then goes on to recommend that this justifies an additional full time role of a 'spare operator'. This individual will need to be a senior operator with sufficient experience to cover absence in any of the operator roles, or, alternatively to relieve someone on the line who can cover the specific absence.

The process line manager and engineer roles are excluded because they are quite distinct skill sets. HR recommends that an additional role of 'developmental process line manager' be created to provide for succession but also for cover across this and other lines within the plant. A similar strategy is recommended for the engineer role.

Scenario 4: modelling to account for demographic change in a volunteer environment.

Perhaps the most difficult workforce environments to manage effectively are those that utilize large numbers of volunteers. Voluntary service is entirely discretionary and these individuals are free to move on, or give up their voluntary work at any time. This leads to a high degree of unpredictability. However, once again, sufficient depth of historical data can ameliorate this uncertainty by describing patterns and trends. Most importantly, good data will allow the manager to achieve a reasonable estimate of what level of staffing is needed to provide the desired level of service. Furthermore, if the organization in question uses volunteers in a number of different roles, it is possible to establish the required ratio of a specific role to the 'customer' base. This ratio can then be set against predicted demographic change in order to develop appropriate recruiting and training strategies.

As an example we will take the case of a regional hospice that operates on the principle of care in the home i.e. it does not operate an in-house palliative care facility. Volunteers of all kinds provide their services to the patient at home. The hospice maintains a corps of full-time employed nurses and a number of management and administration staff. All other services are delivered by volunteers.

A new manager for volunteers has recently taken over and been tasked with developing a volunteer workforce strategy that will account for the inevitable increase in service demand driven by the baby boomers retiring and moving on to the hospice 'radar'. Historically, management of volunteers has been somewhat reactive but this approach is unlikely to meet the certainty of rapidly escalating demand. The manager decides that the time has come to establish clear workforce design principles and to use available data to model volunteer requirements forward through the next 10 years. The underpinning principle is that each volunteer would be recruited, trained and assigned to a primary role. If a volunteer is willing and able to donate time and energy above the requirements of their primary role, this would form part of the contingency for an associated or similar role.

The manager's first tasks are to:

- establish the *status quo* across the range of service provision

- calculate the minimum numbers of volunteers needed to meet the average service demands

- calculate the required contingency based on a general historical average

- calculate the level of risk (to continuity of service) posed by numbers required opposed to numbers actually in place

- factor in increased risk posed by known recruiting difficulties.

- calculate the required ratio (volunteer to patients) in the various roles. This will be essential information for projecting required increases in staffing to align with increasing patient numbers. The ratio is calculated by dividing the total patient number by the rounded up volunteer requirement (which includes the desired contingency).

The spreadsheet below illustrates how this can be done.

Average No patients under care this year.	383
Historic minimum workforce contigency %	40

Volunteer role	No. of vols in place (specific to role)	Number requiring service	Average service delivery (hrs)	Average service repeats	Annualised service delivery requirement	Av No of hours recorded per vol (specific to role)	Min No. vols required (secific to role)	Final total needed	Rounded up requirement	Service delivery risk factor	Risk multiplier (recruiting difficulty) 1-5	Final risk rating	Required ratio Vol to total patient No. (rounded up)
Hairdresser	13	105	2.5	4	1050	85	12.4	17.3	18	133	3	399.1	1 to 22
Manicurist / Pedicurist	9	189	1	4	756	70	10.8	15.1	16	168	3	504	1 to 24
Alt therapy (aroma)	3	46	1.5	2	138	62	2.23	3.12	4	103.9	2	207.74	1 to 96
Alt therapy (massage)	7	245	0.75	5	918.8	85	10.8	15.1	16	216.2	4	864.71	1 to 24
Beautician	6	62	1.5	4	372	50	7.44	10.4	11	173.6	4	694.4	1 to 34
Gardener	8	64	3	6	1152	154	7.48	10.5	11	130.9	2	261.82	1 to 34
Patient Chauffeur	19	311	0.5	12	1866	208	8.97	12.6	13	66.1	1	66.103	1 to 30
Home Handyman	5	26	2	1	52	90	0.58	0.81	1	16.18	1	16.178	1 to 383
Dog Walker	22	65	1	52	3380	254	13.3	18.6	19	84.68	1	84.681	1 to 21
Van driver / equip mover	8	84	1.5	1	126	62	2.03	2.85	3	35.56	2	71.129	1 to 128
Bereavement support	5	24	2	4	192	62	3.1	4.34	5	86.71	3	260.13	1 to 77
Biographer	6	43	1.5	3	193.5	62	3.12	4.37	5	72.82	3	218.47	1 to 77
Photographer	8	102	1	1	102	12	8.5	11.9	12	148.8	4	595	1 to 32

As we have noted on several occasions workforce planning will never be an exact science. Consequently the manager is prepared to proceed on the basis of certain assumptions i.e.

- the level of demand for the various services is fairly constant relative to the number of patients (this is supported by historical data analysis)
- The average number of hours that volunteers are prepared to offer is more or less predictable (again supported by historical data)
- The average time spent on the service delivery and the number of repeat visits is generally predictable.

Column 1 – number of volunteers in place (specific to role). Simple reflection of the status quo. Naturally the numbers tend to be higher for services not requiring high skill levels e.g. dog walking.

Column 2 – number (of patients) that actually accessed the specific service.

Column 3 – average service delivery in hours i.e. how long the volunteers spent on each visit.

Column 4 – number of repeats i.e. how many times the service was requested during the year.

Column 5 – annualized service delivery requirement i.e. the average service delivery x number of repeats x number of patients requesting.

Column 6 – average number of hours recorded by volunteers. This information is critical because it eventually defines the ability of the organization to meet specific service demands.

Column 7 – minimum number (of volunteers) required, at face value, to deliver the specific service i.e. annualized requirement divided by average hours contributed by each volunteer.

Column 8 – Final total needed. This figure adds in the historical contingency requirement (in this case 40%) to produce a number that should mitigate risks associated with primary role holders being unavailable, sick, on holiday etc.

Column 9 – rounded up numbers.

Column 10 – service delivery risk factor, the final total needed divided by the number actually in place x 100. A result of 100 (the risk threshold) indicates a neutral state i.e. the risk is balanced by adequate provision. Results above 100 indicate increasing risk and result below signify decreasing risk.

Column 11 – risk multiplier, a further extrapolation of the risk based on what is known about difficulties in recruiting and bringing up to speed etc. This involves a simple rating scale of 1-5 with 5 being the highest level. The figure at column 10 is multiplied by the 1-5 rating and further highlights the priority roles.

Column 12 – the final risk rating using the 'traffic light' technique.

Column 13 – required ratio, a powerful indicator of the levels that must be maintained as the patient population grows. This is calculated by dividing the number of patients under care by the final total of volunteers required in each role i.e. including contingency.

The next step for the manager is to project forward from the status quo in an attempt to forecast required increases in volunteer manning to align with forecast patient population increases year on year. Historical data reveals that total patients under care sits around 1.6% of the regional 65+ population from which more than 95% of hospice patients are referred. Fortunately, the Regional Authority maintains comprehensive demographic projections for its own planning purposes and this is freely available. Using the annual projections the manager is able to calculate the likely total patient population year on year based on the historical proportion of 1.6% figure. The spreadsheet below performs the calculation and shows patient numbers increasing from 392 to 572. The current levels of service are clearly unsustainable if nothing is done to increase volunteer numbers in a planned manner.

		Regional Plan Forecasts - Population 65+									
Patients average % of regional population 65+	1.60%	2017	2018	2019	2020	2021	2022	2023	2024	2025	2026
		24506	25302	25803	26902	27500	29030	32306	34503	35002	35806
Projected Hospice Patient Population @1.6%		392.1	404.83	412.85	430.43	440	464.48	516.9	552.05	560.03	572.9
Volunteer role	Av. % proportion of patient pop using service	Numbers requiring service (yearly increase)									
Hairdresser	27	105.87	109.3	111.47	116.22	118.8	125.41	139.56	149.05	151.21	154.68
Manicurist / Pedicurist	49	192.13	198.37	202.3	210.91	215.6	227.6	253.28	270.5	274.42	280.72
Alt therapy (aroma)	12	47.052	48.58	49.542	51.652	52.8	55.738	62.028	66.246	67.204	68.748
Alt therapy (massage)	64	250.94	259.09	264.22	275.48	281.6	297.27	330.81	353.31	358.42	366.65
Beautician	16	62.735	64.773	66.056	68.869	70.4	74.317	82.703	88.328	89.605	91.663
Gardener	17	66.656	68.821	70.184	73.173	74.8	78.962	87.872	93.848	95.205	97.392
Patient Chauffeur	81	317.6	327.91	334.41	348.65	356.4	376.23	418.69	447.16	453.63	464.05
Home Handyman	7	27.447	28.338	28.899	30.13	30.8	32.514	36.183	38.643	39.202	40.103
Dog Walker	17	66.656	68.821	70.184	73.173	74.8	78.962	87.872	93.848	95.205	97.392
Van driver / equip mover	22	86.261	89.063	90.827	94.695	96.8	102.19	113.72	121.45	123.21	126.04
Bereavement support	6	23.526	24.29	24.771	25.826	26.4	27.869	31.014	33.123	33.602	34.374
Biographer	11	43.131	44.532	45.413	47.348	48.4	51.093	56.859	60.725	61.604	63.019
Photographer	27	105.87	109.3	111.47	116.22	118.8	125.41	139.56	149.05	151.21	154.68

Using status quo data for the percentage of the patient population requiring each of the volunteer services the manager uses the spreadsheet to project actual demand for the next decade against each of the volunteer roles.

This is very useful information but, more critically, in order to plan, the manager needs to know how the numbers of volunteers needed increase correspondingly. The second half of the spreadsheet shows this aligned extrapolation based on the required ratios. So for example we can see that the current required ratio of hairdressers on call to service the patient population is 18 but this must increase to 27 by 2026 unless volunteers can be prevailed upon to commit more time. This would be a dangerous assumption given that many of the volunteers, such as hairdressers will be employed or running their own businesses.

	Current	2017	2018	2019	2020	2021	2022	2023	2024	2025	2026
Annual projected increase in patient numbers	383	2%	6%	8%	12%	15%	21%	35%	44%	46%	50%
Hairdresser	18	18.36	19.08	19.44	20.16	20.7	21.78	24.3	25.92	26.28	27
Manicurist / Pedicurist	16	16.32	16.96	17.28	17.92	18.4	19.36	21.6	23.04	23.36	25
Alt therapy (aroma)	4	4.08	4.24	4.32	4.48	4.6	4.84	5.4	5.76	5.84	13
Alt therapy (massage)	16	16.32	16.96	17.28	17.92	18.4	19.36	21.6	23.04	23.36	25
Beautician	11	11.22	11.66	11.88	12.32	12.65	13.31	14.85	15.84	16.06	20
Gardener	11	11.22	11.66	11.88	12.32	12.65	13.31	14.85	15.84	16.06	20
Patient Chauffeur	13	13.26	13.78	14.04	14.56	14.95	15.73	17.55	18.72	18.98	22
Home Handyman	1	1.02	1.06	1.08	1.12	1.15	1.21	1.35	1.44	1.46	10
Dog Walker	19	19.38	20.14	20.52	21.28	21.85	22.99	25.65	27.36	27.74	28
Van driver / equip mover	3	3.06	3.18	3.24	3.36	3.45	3.63	4.05	4.32	4.38	12
Bereavement support	5	5.1	5.3	5.4	5.6	5.75	6.05	6.75	7.2	7.3	14
Biographer	5	5.1	5.3	5.4	5.6	5.75	6.05	6.75	7.2	7.3	14
Photographer	12	12.24	12.72	12.96	13.44	13.8	14.52	16.2	17.28	17.52	21

While these figures will never be precise they do provide a feasible window on the future.

The necessity of good data.

It will be clear that workforce planning of this kind, for any scenario, does depend on the availability of rich data. Most organizations of any size will, of necessity, run a human resource information system (HRIS), which should be able to provide a wide range of historical information via interrogation reporting. Young or 'start up' organizations lacking such data will have to make calculated assumptions until data begins to build to meaningful levels.

7

Forecasting supply – managing skills shortages.

"The talent shortage is becoming a reality for a larger number of employers around the world, and this is only going to get worse over the next several decades, as demographic shifts and other factors continue to reduce the number of people who are willing and able to participate in the workforce." Jeffrey Joerres, Chairman & CEO of Manpower Inc. (1).

In recent years, research undertaken by numerous governmental, inter-governmental and commercial organizations (OECD, US Dept. of Labour, CEDEFOP, Hay Group, Manpower Group etc.) has revealed an irony that has left many employers frustrated. Despite many countries having to deal with persistent high levels of unemployment, we are witnessing a shortage of skills critical to economic success across the developed world. Superficially, it is tempting to view this issue as a redeployment problem i.e. we appear to have sufficient people but they are lacking the desired skills sets. Surely all that is needed is to re-train them? Unfortunately, there is a more profound aspect to this problem. We cannot assume that individuals each possess similar capabilities or potential. Those 'other factors' that Jeffrey Joerres refers to above, must include the fact that the contemporary workplace has become more technically challenging and as a consequence we cannot simply assume that the unemployed are able to switch career paths. Capability is fundamentally related to aptitude and, of course intelligence. It is a fact of life that each of us must eventually work within our natural limitations regardless of opportunity. As we move relentlessly from the world of the manual worker to the world of the knowledge worker it is highly likely that an increasing proportion of the potential workforce will be disenfranchised by an inherent lack of capability.

If this situation continues to worsen over the next few decades, HR teams will need to be fully attuned to the local, national and international drivers that shape the workforce and its various motivations.

Those 'other factors' also refer to a number of social and political issues that must eventually be resolved e.g.

- The apparent misalignment, in many countries, between the educational system and actual employer needs. Schools and Universities are now routinely accused of failing to 'produce the goods'. The ongoing demand from employers for a STEM oriented curriculum (Science, Technology, Engineering and Maths) still tends to polarize opinion and confuse the career market place.

- Society, in general, still clings to the notion that a university education, of any kind, is still preferable and more advantageous than qualification in the skilled trades (the old blue collar versus white collar issue).

- Generation X (born between 1960 and 1980) is significantly less numerous than their Baby Boomer predecessors. This means that the proportion of the workforce maturing in skills and experience is shrinking. Thus we see employers looking to the millennials for those characteristics when they may not yet be developed.

- The workforce is generally much more mobile. This means that skilled individuals, in high demand, will be able to demand higher salaries.

- The millennial generation is more inclined to build careers from short-term involvements rather than long term commitment to a single employer. The reality of their world requires them to be 'entrepreneurial' in the management of their careers. Personal development is a critical factor in their decision to stick with a particular employer. Failing to retain key staff is not only damaging, it also fuels the recruitment fires.

So, like it or not, this is a global issue that cannot be ignored. The worsening situation has led increasing numbers of employers to break with simply 'going to the market' in favour of a more flexible approach that includes a range of more proactive tactics. Chief among these is the acceptance that they might need to recruit for potential and then train and develop the individual in house. However, to meet the challenges of talent supply HR departments need to investigate a wider range of alternative tactics and approach the world with fresh thinking. Ironically perhaps, the talent supply challenge may, of necessity, bring about positive re-alignment of traditional thinking and processes and ultimately benefit businesses indirectly.

Talent supply – more flexible tactics.

1. *Expanding recruiting techniques.* The days of simply handing the

recruitment brief to an agency and waiting for the applications to roll in are probably long gone. The battle for critical talent now demands that HR exploits every possible communication channel and every chance for direct contact with 'targeted' individuals. Commonplace techniques now include:

- *Actively researching and maintaining a database of individuals who possess the desired skill sets.* Much can be achieved through the comprehensive mining of professional and social media sites e.g. Linked In and Facebook. Tracking articles in relevant professional journals will also tend to highlight top talent.

- *Making direct approaches to identified individuals* currently employed but not necessarily seeking to move. This can be done through personalized communications packs outlining your business and offering opportunities for on-going contact. Ultimately, any individual will be flattered by being noticed and approached. This may initially be a raising of awareness rather than direct poaching.

- *Looking beyond the obvious discipline and skill set.* Ultimately, it is the raw ingredients of intelligence, drive, passion and willingness to adapt that signal potential success in a role. Recruiters must be prepared to look beyond the obvious sources for high potential individuals who have demonstrated the ability to 'migrate'.

- *Getting beyond the traditional job fair.* This means researching activities in which your target groups engage and getting amongst them. For example, if you are looking for IT staff it is likely that many will show up at a gaming convention. Ensuring that knowledgeable staff attend these events and strike up social relationships will offer opportunities to identify appropriate individuals in an informal setting. Follow-up approaches are then more likely to be received favourably.

- *Improving organizational visibility.* There are numerous tactics for getting noticed e.g. advertising, sponsorship, direct involvement in university or college activities etc. Nevertheless, tunities have arisen with advancing communication technology e.g. use of social media, YouTube and Linked In. Professional associations and institutes will also offer opportunities for organizational self-promotion.

- *Hunting them in their lair.* Find out where your targets like to spend their time, physical and virtual. Make sure you are there with current organizational profiles and links to job vacancies.

- *Maximizing the referral.* Use your existing employees to put the word out through their personal networks. Consider a 'reward' scheme for successful referrals.

- *Reviewing previously declined candidates.* Never forget that circumstances change. The candidate you declined three years ago may have gained experience and developed new skills that would now make her a very good fit for the role you need to fill.

- *Running 'open house' events.* Well promoted open days with clear indications of subsequent hiring opportunities will attract those who are really interested in your organization or the business sector. This will focus your recruiting on the most highly motivated.

2. *Organizational review.* As Henry Ford was fond of saying "if you always do what you've always done, you'll get what you always got". The lesson here is clear enough. If you cannot get the expertise you need to fill a role in its present form, you may need to re-think the way things are done. For example, is it possible to break the role open and re-allocate or exchange some functions sufficiently to allow you to look for a rather different candidate?

Is it possible to re-examine work flow or to look at investment in technology to eradicate the need for specific expertise? Is it possible to re-align departments so that existing expertise can more effectively cover the gap?

3. Re-evaluate existing personnel. Few organizations maintain or even initiate in-depth skills / experience inventories of their staff. Other than what is exhibited in their current roles, so much latent talent flies under the radar. Essentially this is a failing of management to fully appreciate (and utilize) its talent pool. In today's environment this is negligence of a high order. So often, the solution is to be found in the back yard. Understanding our people in depth may allow us to recognize those who have the potential to be developed and migrated into more critical roles, leaving a simpler recruitment task in terms of their original role replacement.

4. *Grow your own.* Most organizations are coming to terms with the fact that the market place is increasingly unable to provide required expertise in any reliable manner. So, if your pipes burst and you can't get a plumber, you need to fix it yourself or suffer the consequences. Traditionally, of course, many businesses have adopted the 'grow your own' strategy for their tradesmen and front line operators e.g. through apprenticeships and on-job training for progression. Where these strategies have been abandoned (mostly for political reasons) we have seen industry suffer significantly. With some notable exceptions, internal development has not generally been the case for the professions or for management. It is only in recent years that we have seen the emergence of the 'pipeline' concept for internal leadership development (2).

Buying in talent will always be a major strategy and, of course, fresh blood entering the gene pool is always a positive. What emerges now is that this should not be relied upon as the major strategy for succession. Internal development processes may be intimidating for smaller organizations that lack sufficient resource or expertise to develop and sustain formal training coaching and mentoring systems to fill the gap. In these situations they must look to independent support systems to provide the scaffolding and standards required. This support usually emerges in the form of governmental training and qualification structures initiatives, tertiary education programmes or perhaps initiatives driven by industry groups, associated professional institutes or representative bodies.

The obvious potential advantage of a 'grow your own' strategy is that you stand a much better chance of getting exactly what you want. Relying on external provision e.g. through educational establishments, private training providers etc. will inevitably mean some sacrifice to generic considerations. The obvious disadvantage is that 'grow your own' requires some degree of internal resource and expertise to design, build and sustain development systems. On a small scale this can be very informal e.g. a single apprentice being taken on and assigned to an 'old hand' for training. This approach will not work for larger scale organizations which will be much more dependent on structure and management systems. In these situations, most organizations will look for some kind of learning and development framework to assure predictability of skills provision. Stand-alone internal frameworks are comparatively rare because they are dependent on sustained commitment from management and the workforce in terms of resources, expertise and the willingness of everybody to participate. Furthermore, experience shows that staff, at all levels, place more value on training or educational activity that is externally credentialed. An increasingly mobile workforce places a premium on qualifications that are readily transferable. This factor most often leads to the linking of internal systems to external frameworks and the creation of collaborative partnerships.

A successful "Grow Your Own" strategy will of course depend on the determined use of techniques such as Markov analysis (see page 77) and the commitment of management to developmental tactics.

5. *Partnerships and collaboration.*

Any organization that seeks to build a capability 'pipeline' would be wise to seeks assistance wherever it may be found. The majority of developed countries will have evolved a complex of support systems that can offer various kinds of direct and indirect assistance. The table below shows a typical inter-related hierarchy.

Potential Partner / Collaboration	Nature of support
Government.	Over-arching policy frameworks. Funding mechanisms.
Qualifications Authorities.	Governance of transferable skills standards. Maintenance of national qualifications frameworks. Advice on assessment methods. Register of approved training providers.
Educational establishments. Colleges, polytechnics and universities.	Provision of generic qualification programmes to established learning levels (usually aligned to national qualification framework descriptors). May offer opportunities for unique relationships.
Industry Training Organisations. Bodies representing specific industry sectors.	Forums for industry groups to work together to identify needs and build mutually advantageous training systems – usually aligned to transferable qualifications.
Vocational Training (VET) establishments.	Training establishments focused entirely on delivery of job-related skills.
Private training enterprises.	Mixed provision of short course vocational training, core skills, lower level management / supervisory skills etc.

Unions / staff representative bodies.	Essential 'moral' support for training initiatives. Guidance on what the workforce actually values.
Consultants.	Specific technical advice and design input for systems and content.
Professional Institutes / Bodies.	Guidance on professional standards and associated training related to the profession.

So, for those organizations that choose to develop internal systems or to align to an established qualification structure, the spectrum of potential support is somewhat bewildering. Where specific L&D expertise is lacking this responsibility will probably falls to general HR and it is certainly advisable to approach a consultancy for assistance with answering the following key questions.

- Where are my biggest risks? Which roles need a guaranteed capability pipeline?
- How do I identify the specific learning content for each role?
- How do I identify the learning level that should be achieved?
- Can / should these learning interventions be aligned to external transferable qualifications?
- What would the costs be? Can I get some kind of support funding from government or industry sources?
- How could we deliver this learning? Would it be all on-job, a mix of on-job, off-job, on-line etc?
- If I need to involve external providers how do I identify the good ones?
- What kind of governance systems do I need to establish to make this work?
- What internal resources will I need to set tis up and keep it going? Will senior management support it?
- How do I make sure this aligns with the organizational culture and values?
- What are the change management implications?

Perhaps the most valuable advice and support will come from other organizations in the industry sector that have already travelled this path or are well down the road. Direct contact and cooperation between HR departments may be possible where there is no obvious competition issue. Alternatively, industry training organizations or federations may have established forums through which this kind of support is available. Perhaps as a last resort enquiries could be made to the relevant government ministry?

Implementing learning and development initiatives is never easy. Creating a comprehensive framework or system will be a long term affair, accompanied by frequent setbacks. Fortunately there are proven models freely available. For example, sound advice can be found at the Australian Public Service web site. (3) The principles outlined here can easily be adapted to most organizations.

Exploiting the whole workforce.

Historically, organizations tend to build recruiting traditions, many of them stemming from the very partnerships recommended above. Then potential drawback to this is that traditions may evolve into straitjackets, blinkering management and closing off rich sources of talent.

HR professionals must now encourage their businesses to look again at who and how it brings new blood into the critical roles. The categories that must now be explored more fully are:

- *Women* – the age of the male as the designated 'breadwinner' has largely disappeared but there are still cultures (e.g. Japan) where the vast resource of female capability is largely untapped. Even in the more 'enlightened' nations, glass ceilings prevent women fulfilling their full potential. This doesn't just disadvantage women, it puts culprit organizations directly into harm's way. (4)

- *Minorities* – diversity in the workforce has been shown, quite convincingly, to enrich and empower organizations. People from the minority groups invariably bring with them different perspectives and can positively help with continuing transformation.
- *The disabled* – physical disability does not necessarily equate to mental impairment. Work and workplaces can be re-engineered to allow those who might struggle otherwise to contribute and give of their best. (5)
- *Older workers* – there is little disagreement now, we just have to find ways of encouraging and enabling people to work on beyond the 'normal' age of retirement – as long as they add value. (6)

References.

1. Available at:
http://manpowergroup.com/talent-shortage-2016

2. See Charan, R, Drotter, S. Noel, J. (2001 revised 2011). *The Leader ship Pipeline.* Wiley & Son.

3. See *Building Capability: A Framework for Managing Learning & Development in the Australian Public Service.* (2003). Available at: *http://www.apsc.gov.au/__data/assets/pdf_file/0008/50975/capabilit y.pdf*

4. See *Women at Work –Trends 2016.* International Labour Office Geneva. available at: *https://www.cliclavoro.gov.it/Barometro-Del-Lavoro/Documents/2016/ILO_women_at_work_2016.pdf*

5. See *Market Research Report: Making the Case for Hiring and Retaining People with Disabilities*. Cornell University, GladNet Collection. available at:

http://digitalcommons.ilr.cornell.edu/cgi/viewcontent.cgi?article=141 0&context=gladnetcollect

6. See *A New Vision for Older Workers: Retain, Retrain, Recruit*. Report to the UK Government. Available at:

http://www.legco.gov.hk/general/english/library/stay_informed_overs eas_policy_updates/a_new_vision_for_older_workers.pdf

8

Do we need a software solution?

A cursory Google search for 'workforce planning software' will return hundreds of hits, leading us to believe that the field is highly developed. However, a second glance reveals that the majority of these tools are no more than scheduling or rostering devices and are thus more closely related to workforce *deployment*. While useful in themselves, they do not provide an easy, automated perspective on the capability and capacity required in a given workforce.

Software solutions that attempt to do this have certainly been developed and made available but, in our VUCA world, we must inevitably be somewhat sceptical of their reliability? They also come at a considerable cost and HR departments must therefore be convinced of the validity of their application before presenting a business case for acquisition. Many of these solutions attempt to integrate numerous metrics in order to alleviate inevitable stochastical tendencies. It could be argued that a simpler approach provides sufficient (and more accessible) clarity. As Sinclair puts it:

Most organizations and most planning situations do not require a complicated technique or complicated software. Except for a few organizations that allow it, it is unlikely that organizations will use complex statistical models because the environment is too unstable and cannot specify demand with any precision. Whilst the software pack-ages tend to offer a number of benefits besides workforce planning, they are often expensive and HR software is frequently reported as being difficult to use. According to Reilly, they are also surplus to the requirements of the workforce planning activity. Simple spreadsheet models, tailor-made and based on accurate and complete data are all that is required. (1)

This statement agrees wholeheartedly with the fundamental tenet of this book i.e. that workforce planning can, and should be, a relatively simple process, well within the capability of the HR department, using readily available data and simple, context relevant, custom built tools. That much said we should not discount generic software solutions available to those organizations able to afford and support them.

Many of the software tools presenting themselves as workforce plan-ning solutions are in fact primarily focused on workforce *management* e.g. tasks such as scheduling and deployment. As such, they are essen-tially red / green horizon planning tools and undoubtedly valuable providing they are supported by expert use and good data. The GIGO rule (garbage in – garbage out) always applies. Which system you se-lect will depend on precise business needs and the ability to interface with current systems. Given that these solutions tend to be very ex-pensive, the assistance of a competent business analyst is advisable. There are various websites that offer comparison charts and these are useful in narrowing down the field e.g. *SelectHub* and *FinancesOnLine*.

As Reilly indicates above, we should be sceptical regarding software solutions for blue horizon planning. In practice, the HR professional, in possession of intimate knowledge of the organization and effective scenario modeling from the senior management team should be able to achieve adequate results with simple 'home made' tools using simple logical processes.

"Claiming a piece of software can provide a full talent management system is a bit like claiming that a food processor will produce a 5 star meal. These tools are valuable in support of a good plan or recipe. The right tools clear the path for smoother execution and may improve the end product. But tools mean nothing without the right expertise and the right ingredients behind them." (2)

References.

1. Sinclair. A. (2004). Workforce Planning – a literature review. IES Research Networks. Page 8
2. Wellins R. Smith, A. Erker, S. (2009). *Nine Best Practices for Effective Talent Management.* DDI White paper. Page 12.

Index

About the author.

Brian is a learning and development professional with some 40 years of wide-ranging experience. Much of that time has been spent attached to the UK Ministry of Defence where he was employed in a specialist training and development role across all three armed services, but primarily with the Army.

After leaving Defence in 1995 he worked in a freelance capacity in the UK on educational projects in the tertiary education sector and assisted industry and emergency services with the design of internal assessment systems. In 1998 Brian moved to New Zealand with his family and took up a post with the newly created training support division of the New Zealand Fire Service. Working initially on the creation of new training programmes he was selected to project manage an initiative aimed at the complete rebuild of the Service's training and progression system.

Moving on from the Fire Service he worked independently as a consultant, focusing particularly on the design, development and delivery of leadership and management skills training in New Zealand and across the South Pacific.

In 2011 Brian took up his present post as Head of Learning and Development for an Australasian Pulp & Paper Company. He is currently working on the introduction of the Systems Approach to Training and the enhancement of leadership capability across the business. Integral to the systems approach are the workforce planning techniques described in this book.

CPSIA information can be obtained at www.ICGtesting.com
Printed in the USA
LVIW01n1327200318
570499LV00001B/10